Three-dimensional
Embroidery

Three-dimensional Embroidery

Methods of construction for
the third dimension

Janet Edmonds

Batsford

ISBN 0 7134 8965 0

A CIP catalogue record for this book is available from the
British Library.

Printed in China
for the Publishers
B T Batsford
The Chrysalis Building
Bramley Road
London W10 6SP
www.chrysalisbooks.co.uk

An imprint of **Chrysalis** Books Group plc

Photography by Michael Wicks unless otherwise stated.

Acknowledgements

My grateful thanks go to my family for putting up with 'the book'
for so long, and who have had to learn to fend for themselves while
I was preoccupied. Appreciation in particular goes to my sons, Tim
and Ben, who have helped and supported me with endless patience,
whilst I grappled with computer skills and struggled with design
decisions. I am indebted to my talented students who have so
generously and willingly lent me their beautiful work to illustrate
the book, and to friends for their encouragement and support.
I thank you all. Finally, my thanks go to Helen Evans at Batsford for
her help and guidance, for making sense of the muddle that has
become the book.

Contents

INTRODUCTION 7

1. DESIGN 10
The design brief 12
Research: gathering information 12
Thinking time 15
Selecting a starting point 16
The design process 18

2. MATERIALS AND EQUIPMENT 24
Materials 24
Tools and equipment 29

3. CONSTRUCTING WITH FLAT PIECES 34
Geometrics 35
Free form 50

4. CONTINUOUS LENGTHS 54
Coiling 54
Free-form building with continuous lengths 65

5. MANIPULATED METHODS 70
Fabrics 72
Manipulative techniques 74
Working with a former 90

6. BEADS 94
Soft beads 96
Hard beads 102
Building with beads 108

7. FINISHING TECHNIQUES 116
Edges and rims 116
Bases, supports and feet 118
Lids 122

CONCLUSION 124

RESOURCES 126

INDEX 128

Introduction

We live in a three-dimensional world where everything in it fits together like a jigsaw, with height, width and depth. We take this for granted and usually accept the knowledge of what we see without question. We know that everything is three-dimensional, and that small items can be picked up and turned around and can be moved from place to place, altering the visual picture and changing the relationship of one thing to another. We can walk into a 'scene' and look around, behind, up and down, and to each side, experiencing different views of the same objects.

This knowledge offers endless scope for design and can be much more exciting and challenging than two-dimensional design where the images have only height and width. It is, however, more complex having to consider the third dimension, namely depth, especially when working on a two-dimensional surface. Only one view can be seen in any one drawing, so a number of drawings need to be made to understand the whole object. The design process may be transformed by 'drawing' in three dimensions, that is, making models or maquettes. Working drawings in the round makes it possible to understand what is happening with spatial relationships and it is much easier to make adjustments. Additional elements can be added without having to make lots of drawings with the need for perspective.

Looking back into the history of British and world embroidery, there are well-established traditions for three-dimensional, embroidered artefacts. Centuries ago, in all regions of the world, function and need were usually the purpose for their existence, but as cultures became more complex, so too did the garments, bags, boxes and all the other items required for both secular and religious life. There is a wealth of inspiration here and it is fascinating to see the styles and methods change as needs and fashions come and go.

Within the culture of the West, for example, the Elizabethan period of English history, with its richly embroidered surfaces, has elaborate costumes of cloth of gold and comforts for the home, with cushions and pillows intricately stitched. Accessories included small bags and purses, ruffs, gauntlets and shoes. Then, during the 17th century,

LEFT: Fabric is pieced with applied strips of fine material and tucks are stitched across to vary the direction. The lining is formed from cotton organdie, and is tucked in the same way. The two fabrics combine to give an interesting contrast between the texture on the inside and outside of the item – a contrast often found in the natural world of plants. Irregular-shaped pieces of cloth are seamed together to create the shape. The edge is simply bound with fabric.

stumpwork boxes became fashionable. These small table cabinets, used for toilet articles, writing materials or as needlework boxes, were made from wood and decorated with biblical, classical or allegorical pictures worked in raised embroidery, with coloured silks on white satin. The human figures within the panels depict the elaborate fashions of the Stuart court, surrounded by animals, insects, birds and buildings all worked in high relief, and were the intricate work of young girls as a show of their needlework skills.

The 18th century saw very elaborate costume for both men and women, and stitched coverings for furniture added to domestic comfort. During the Victorian period there was a fashion for a wide range of needlework and craft projects. The American magazine, *Godey's Lady's Book*, was first published in 1838 in Philadelphia and it encouraged women everywhere to make decorative items for the home to satisfy every conceivable use. The magazine included a 'fancy work department' and gave instructions for these household items in each issue. Lampshades, picture frames, workbaskets and jewellery cases, boxes to contain collars and cuffs, cigars, shoes or sewing accessories proliferated. Artificial flowers were very popular and these were made from a variety of materials including paper, silk, feathers, leather and beads. Nothing was too humble to be decorated. There were even instructions for an embroidered penwiper, which was probably a very important and necessary requirement for 19th-century ladies.

Much later, during the second half of the 20th century, there was great ingenuity with all manner of themes inspiring non-functional work. During the early 1970s, for example, there was a trend towards soft sculpture, with food being a popular subject. Possibly the influence of Pop Art encouraged the idea of everyday imagery as inspiration for embroidery. Sandwiches, cakes and pastries, fruit and vegetables, gardens and life-size figures were all made with fabric and thread in three dimensions. Abstract pieces using manipulated techniques were large and architectural in style. American Ed Rossbach influenced a new approach to traditional basketry and weaving. This promoted many fresh avenues for exploring the making of vessels and containers using mixed media, some functional, some not.

These are just a few examples from history of the many and varied three-dimensional, mostly functional, items that may inspire contemporary work, but it is not my intention, in this book, to deal with function as a primary requirement of an artefact. There are very many excellent books on the market that specialize in the making of functional items, such as bags and boxes, garments and accessories. Neither is it my intention to deal with the techniques of decorative surface textures, as these aspects of embroidery are also well catered for.

In this book, I intend to explore form by approaching the design of three-dimensional items, through techniques of building and shaping in various ways without the constraint of function, although that is not to rule function out as a possible outcome. The ideas that are presented may be further developed and adapted to functional items. Where possible, suggestions are made as to how the ideas may be used.

It is often the case that when the design of an item is considered, a two-dimensional method is used, such as a flat drawing or sketch on paper. I present some methods and processes that take the image off the drawing board and into space, so that the maker is inspired, and led to consider, the third dimension of depth when designing.

Whether working with the discipline of geometrics or with the freedom of free-form building, I hope to show that it is possible to create complex structures that may be adapted for a variety of three-dimensional items, and to inspire readers to experiment with processes and to combine them with decorative surfaces that are integral to the form.

Chapter 1
Design

While the building blocks of design are colour, shape and pattern, line, texture and form, it is the combination of these, together with an enquiring attitude of mind and the willingness to experiment, that can bring about exciting and original pieces of work. While there is an established sequence of stages to work through, individuals must make their own personal journey to find the methods and processes that suit them and their ideas. Some like to record information in the form of drawings to discover the essence of their theme and others prefer to explore through experimenting with materials. It is also worth combining these approaches and working through them in tandem. It makes sense to follow whatever method brings results for you and gives you the necessary buzz of creativity.

In the consideration of three-dimensional items, form and structure are usually of primary importance, with colour and surface pattern playing a supporting role. These can come later when consideration has been given to the structure, scale and material strength of the piece. There may, however, be exceptions to this. An example might be when making work that relies on the effect of light. In this case, the type and colour of the material will be important and should be considered at an earlier stage.

So, where do the ideas come from? And where do you start?

BELOW AND RIGHT: Dried morel mushrooms have an intriguing texture of pockets and ridges. Each tiny shape forms a perfect vessel and inspired the piece opposite.

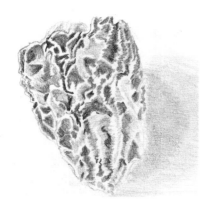

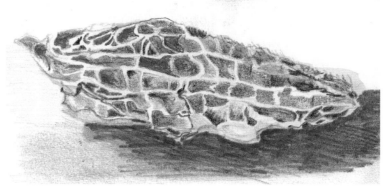

The design brief

In order to create new ideas and fresh ways of thinking, it is necessary to gather as much information about your subject as you can. Identify the problem to be solved and research it. Find out as much as possible, so that you are familiar with the subject and can work from the point of knowledge. Original ideas do not just appear as if by magic. There is a process to be followed and, to begin with, looking, gathering and recording information is the first priority. Using this information to create designs can then follow by selecting, choosing and experimenting with placing and arranging.

Research – gathering information

One method of recording ideas is to keep a sketchbook. Drawing is an important and necessary part of the creative process, being a good way of learning about your subject, and should be considered as widely as possible. Detailed drawings, as well as rough sketches, writing notes and mark making with a range of media to suggest ideas and inspiration, and photographs or magazine cuttings, are all useful methods of building a picture and understanding your subject. Recording the journey and progress of a piece of work from its initial conception through to its conclusion is a valuable process, and enables you to track ideas and trends and to resolve problems.

BELOW LEFT: Drawings based on Bertel Badger's book *Nature as Designer* show many types of plant structures that can be examined when studying seeds and pods for three-dimensional work. I have been inspired by these plants for many years, first as a potter and now as an embroiderer.

BELOW CENTRE: The cage of veins is all that is left of the campanula, or bellflower, once the soft matter has crumbled away.

BELOW RIGHT: This drawing of a datura flower suggests ruched fabric or pleats.

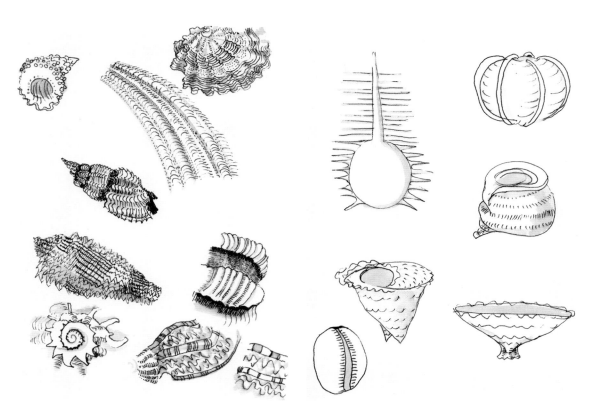

ABOVE LEFT: Shells of molluscs are a perennial favourite as a source of inspiration. Some are so small that a magnifying glass is needed to appreciate their intricate details. Close inspection reveals tiny, delicate marks in a vast array of patterns.

ABOVE RIGHT: Shells are found in lots of different shapes and sizes, and the spiral pattern on the shell is often integral to its design.

RIGHT: Subtle colour schemes are found on shells when they are examined closely. Try recording the proportion of colours found. A palette of soft faded pinks and yellows are enhanced with some very pale cream and a tiny amount of strong brown or terracotta.

To make an observational drawing, you will need to look very closely at the subject. Normally, in the course of going about our daily business, we skim across the surface of things, taking for granted the relative position of one thing to another. Colour is a blur and surface detail, in most cases, often goes unnoticed. It needs a conscious effort to take proper account of what we see. Every now and then, our attention is alerted to something, and we stop and begin to look more closely. Usually, though, it takes a prompt of some sort for this to happen. Observational drawing requires close scrutiny and takes time and effort, but there is no better way to really get to know your subject.

So, what information is important? In a three-dimensional context, form, structure and space should be identified in the first instance, with colour and surface of secondary importance. If you can pick up the source of inspiration, handle it and experience it directly through touch, it is possible to understand more about it. The properties of the material it is made from may be hard and strong, soft and flexible, or delicate and fragile. These combine with the object itself, giving structure, weight, balance and scale. Spaces within it are defined by boundaries, while light and tone may help to define shape and structure.

Consider the shape or shapes, positive and negative, and how they fit together. Does one shape dominate? What is around it and how does it relate to the surroundings and the background? Can you see inside the form and how does it blend or contrast with the outside surface? Is it angular and geometric or is it organic with flowing lines and curving surfaces? What effect does light have, and what is the range of tonal values? What kind of surface do you see; rough, smooth, knobbly, spiky or hairy? Imagine that you are describing the object to someone who cannot see it and record as much information as you can, noting things that may be helpful later on when you are ready to move forward into the design stage.

Draw your subject several times using a range of methods and media. Change the viewpoint or angle of vision. It is a good idea to become familiar with tools and media. You need to know what kind of marks on paper you can get from pencils, pens and paint, and what tools to use to achieve a particular effect. Give yourself permission to play with the media that you have at your disposal so that you can record more effectively what you see. This information, when meticulously recorded, is invaluable when looking for ideas to take forward into design development for finished pieces.

Thinking time

This is often overlooked, but time to mull over ideas, toss them around, discuss with like-minded friends, is invaluable. It gives you the freedom to imagine all kinds of possibilities, which may or may not be worth following up.

Looking at familiar objects in unfamiliar ways can begin to open up new avenues of investigation and creative thought. Thinking 'outside the box' means to think the unthinkable and to suggest the ridiculous. To illustrate this, it is useful to create a mind map to stimulate ideas because when you see these recorded on the page it is often possible to see similarities or to make comparisons. Out of this can develop connections between things that you hadn't seen before and new arrangements or patterns can emerge that previously were not obvious.

This process inevitably requires some degree of risk taking that can be uncomfortable because you don't know what the result will be.

BELOW: Drawing a mind map can be a useful method of recording a train of thought about a subject. Set down on paper anything and everything that you can think of about your key word, however obscure it may sound. Seeing the words on paper can often help you to make connections between areas of information that are not immediately obvious.

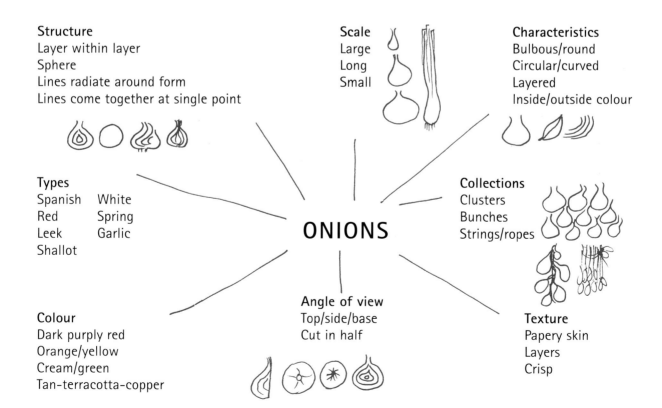

Structure
Layer within layer
Sphere
Lines radiate around form
Lines come together at single point

Types
Spanish   White
Red   Spring
Leek   Garlic
Shallot

Colour
Dark purply red
Orange/yellow
Cream/green
Tan-terracotta-copper

Scale
Large
Long
Small

ONIONS

Angle of view
Top/side/base
Cut in half

Characteristics
Bulbous/round
Circular/curved
Layered
Inside/outside colour

Collections
Clusters
Bunches
Strings/ropes

Texture
Papery skin
Layers
Crisp

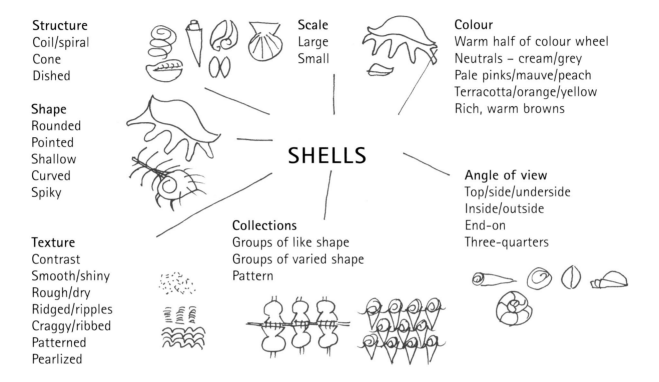

Structure
Coil/spiral
Cone
Dished

Shape
Rounded
Pointed
Shallow
Curved
Spiky

Texture
Contrast
Smooth/shiny
Rough/dry
Ridged/ripples
Craggy/ribbed
Patterned
Pearlized

Scale
Large
Small

SHELLS

Collections
Groups of like shape
Groups of varied shape
Pattern

Colour
Warm half of colour wheel
Neutrals – cream/grey
Pale pinks/mauve/peach
Terracotta/orange/yellow
Rich, warm browns

Angle of view
Top/side/underside
Inside/outside
End-on
Three-quarters

But the aim is to move away from familiar experience and stereotypical thinking, and to achieve new and innovative ideas based on the ordinary and commonplace.

ABOVE: A mind map based on the subject of shells.

Selecting a starting point

When you have enough observational material you can move forward to the next stage, and this is to explore design ideas on paper.

Starting points for creative thinking might take the form of selecting a part of a drawing rather than using all of it. Remove parts of the subject to subtract something from the whole. The subject could be repeated or duplicated or expanded in some way. Separate objects, alike or dissimilar, could be brought together and arranged in a new mix, perhaps repeated. The repeat may be to take one shape and repeat it many times, randomly or in a more organized way, or to repeat the shape but change the size of it.

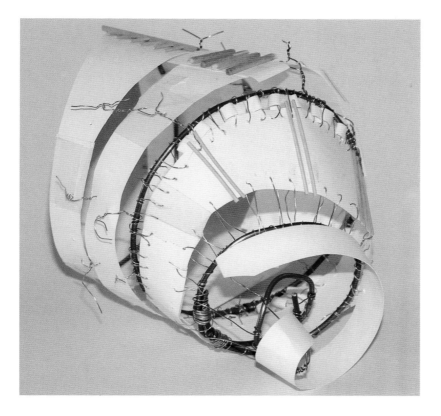

ABOVE: The surface markings found on some shells that could inspire a three-dimensional interpretation.

BELOW: These drawings with simplified marks were used to build a model that shows what happens all around the shape without being restricted to only one view.

LEFT: Thick wire is bent into a spiral, and finer wire used in the spaces. Paper strips coil around the shape and the surface texture is recreated with matchsticks.

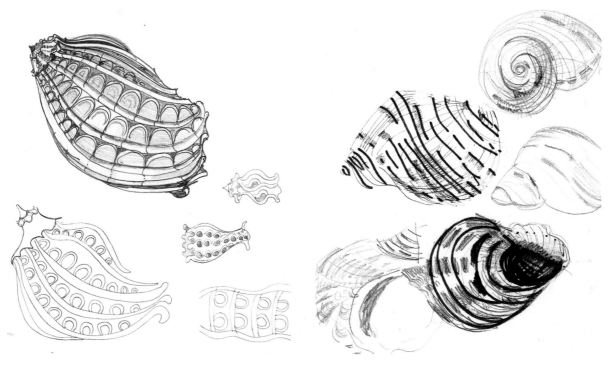

Adding another element to the subject creates different connections. Put the subject in a new and unfamiliar context that may alter the balance or focus of the subject, and make it look different and so suggest further development. Changing the viewpoint by looking from above, from below or from an unusual angle, may give a new slant on a design. Another idea is to randomly select two different drawings and combine them, perhaps drawing one directly over the other or using an overlay. Move it about to see what effect it has on the drawing beneath. Redraw to make a new image.

I find that if I use tone in a very definite way, so that I have some strong contrasts in a drawing, it will often suggest a dimensional interpretation.

The design process

There will come a point when it becomes necessary to take the drawings off the sketchbook page and move into three dimensions. Models and mock-ups are essential for exploring the structure in the round. Only then can you judge the mass and volume, and see whether it is balanced. It is easier to see how the chosen material will support the form and to make adjustments to angles, viewpoints and scale. You can see immediately whether the form is stable and is strong enough to support itself. It is possible to identify the areas that need strengthening and reduce those that are too heavy.

It is useful to consider how Nature deals with design. Peter Stevens tells us in his book, *Patterns in Nature*, that 'Nature thickens areas of high stress, adds reinforcement between top and bottom plates and leaves areas of low stress paper thin'. He also says that the 'stratagem of design is the reduction of mass in order to increase strength'. The two methods that Nature and Humankind have adapted and used to overcome the effects of increasing size are either to use a stronger material or to make the structure hollow and reduce its weight. Any material will eventually break under its own weight, so the solution seems to be to arrange the material differently. It can be cut away where it is not needed and be thickened where more strength is required. This process can be seen in the use of ribbed constructions, box sections, space frames, T-beams, folded plates and trusses. Many of these solutions are used by architects designing buildings, but they are as relevant for embroiderers working three-dimensionally. All are methods of

FACING PAGE
RIGHT: Observational drawings of onions using pen and ink.

BELOW RIGHT: Simplified shapes have been developed from observational drawings, which in turn have been interpreted as a card model. Size, proportion and structure can be addressed and the shape viewed from all angles.

BELOW LEFT:
A paper model developed from drawings and designs of red onions. A hat block was used to support the shape created from strips of thick paper, with a cardboard tube to form the neck.

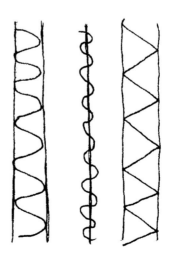

ABOVE: Methods of reinforcing.

BELOW: The outside leaves of a sweetcorn husk have been machine-stitched together to form a delicate structure. The leaves are flexible when they are green but, as they dry out, the shape shrinks and twists to form a more complex shape.

ABOVE AND TOP LEFT: Horse chestnuts
that have just fallen from a tree in
autumn. They were first sewn together
when they were still soft and green.
As they dry, they become more flexible
and can be draped over a support to give
further ideas. An observational drawing is
shown on the facing page.

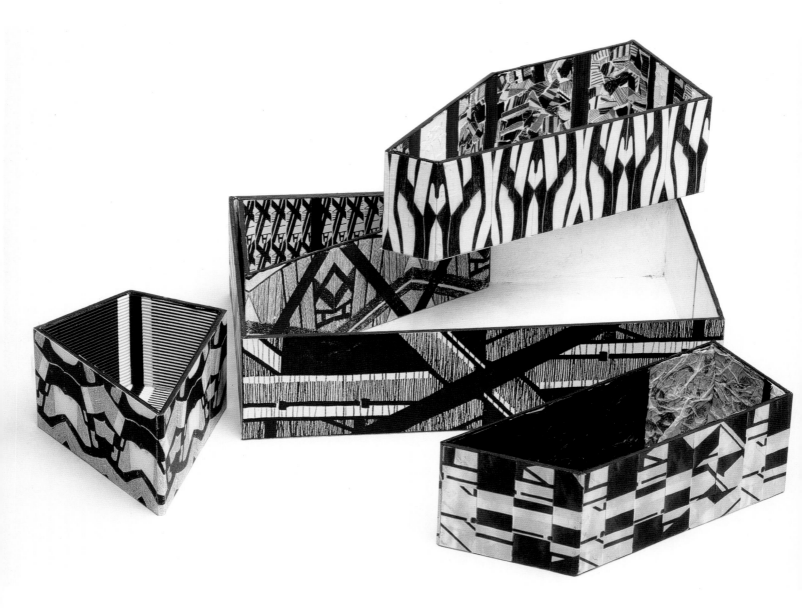

ABOVE: This set of black and white boxes was developed from pencil drawings of bridges and lock-winding equipment. The drawings were scanned, manipulated and resized on a computer to fit the outer surfaces. The inside of the boxes are decorated with various textures that reflect this theme. (Anne Davies)

reducing the mass of material while leaving enough in place to create a strong structure. A good example would be the construction of corrugated cardboard. By sandwiching a ridged layer between two flat ones you have a light but strong material. Many manipulative techniques produce ridged surfaces that are stronger than a flat piece of fabric. The problem to solve is choosing the best technique method to realize your design.

Evaluating what you have made can be really useful as it forces you to be objective. Consider the result of your mock-up and, if it isn't what you want, adjust it. If function is important you will need to test this and work out what the criteria should be. If, for example, you are making a lampshade, be sure that your design will let enough light out, that it is a stable structure and the material will withstand the heat of a bulb without melting or burning.

When you are satisfied that your idea is going to work and decisions about form are resolved, consideration can be given to colour and surface. Although these are important to the work, it is essential that they complement the design and do not look like an afterthought. Make sure that any surface decoration is integral to the design and remove anything that is superfluous. As Goethe said, 'there is nothing superfluous about good design'.

The completed design may suggest a technique or method of making, but it is a good idea to explore a range of fabrics to discover their suitability for your design. What you thought would work may not, so be prepared to try out your ideas in fabric and make some samples.

The following chapters explore methods of building that could be carried out in a variety of materials. By changing the qualities of the fabric, a different look or feel can be created. A light, transparent quality could be achieved with organdie or fine silk, but a more robust design might be better constructed out of felt or canvas.

Chapter 2
Materials and equipment

This chapter describes some commonly used materials and equipment that may be needed for three-dimensional work. Local hardware shops and DIY stores can be good places to look for some of the items listed rather than an embroidery outlet, but specialist suppliers may also need to be sought out for more hard-to-find materials and equipment. It is also possible to source most things through the Internet, given a little time and patience.

The usual range of fabrics and threads, needles and a sewing machine are needed, and more detailed information about these items will be given throughout the book where appropriate.

Materials

It is often worth considering the humblest of materials. With a little ingenuity surprising results can be achieved. Many local authorities now run recycling schemes, commonly known as scrap stores, where all kinds of items can be acquired, from waste card to plastics and computer parts. The good thing about such schemes is that you can pick up small items in quantity if you need repeats of them, or long lengths of wire or nylon thread. You can take back what you don't use and substitute other things instead. It is a system that is well worth investigating.

FABRICS
Vilene is a non-woven interfacing normally used for dressmaking. It comes in a range of thicknesses and types. I have found the craft weight type most useful for construction for its properties of strength, ease of cutting and shaping, but the variety used for soft furnishing purposes, which has an iron-on surface, is useful too.

Vilene can be dyed with cold-water dyes, although it is only possible to achieve a mid tone, as it is a man-made material. It is good with transfer dyes and for painting with acrylic or emulsion paints. It can support other fabrics by stitching or bonding and can be

RIGHT AND BELOW: Stage felt was used here to form a vessel inspired by a drawing of rocks, shown below.

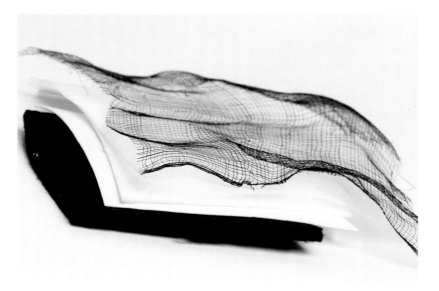

manipulated by folding, rolling and pleating. As it is non-woven, it will not fray and gives a crisp edge when cut.

Other fabrics include:

- **Felt** – wool, acrylic, viscose or industrial types normally used for the stage.
- **Hessian** – a loosely woven fabric that can be easily manipulated.
- **Leather** – strong; useful for binding edges or for adding strength to vulnerable areas; gives clean, crisp edges when cut.
- **Sinemay** – a woven natural fibre, often used for making hats.

THREADS
Strong linen thread can be used to bind elements together and will stand a fair amount of tension. Nymo thread is designed for beading, is very strong and available in a range of colours, as well as black and white.

WOOD
Wood is a useful material as it is relatively easy to work with. Holes are easily drilled into it. It can be cut and sanded, then polished, dyed or painted with a huge variety of paints and polishes. Many types, sizes and lengths of shaped mouldings can be found in DIY stores and some suppliers will cut wood to size if you need a piece as a base or support for your textile.

ABOVE: Thick rope or string can be dyed, wrapped or used as a stuffing. Continuous lengths can be woven to create form and structure.

ABOVE LEFT: Some fabrics are particularly useful when creating three-dimensional work, particularly stage felt, Vilene and sinemay.

Balsa wood, found in specialist hobby shops, can be very easily cut and shaped. It is lightweight and soft enough to pass thread or wire through with a large needle or through drilled holes.

Cocktail sticks and barbeque sticks can be used to join sections together or to divide one section from another. They can be passed through a channel stitched into fabric to give support.

WIRE

Wire comes in many forms, not only in lengths, but also as meshes and sheets. It is usually measured in millimetres or by weight in grams and is available in copper, steel, silver, aluminium and galvanized. The types of wires or metals normally used by embroiderers are at the fine to medium end of the spectrum, unless of course they are working at a very large scale. Some wires are coloured and available through specialist jewellery suppliers. If your budget is tight, a trip to your local waste-disposal site or recycling centre may be worthwhile as they often sell copper and other wires and metals very cheaply. Wires may be treated by annealing, soldering, twisting or flattening, and fine-gauge wires are easily cut with tin snips or scissors.

Wire as a support can be pushed into holes drilled into wood, threaded through tubular ribbon or perhaps bound or sewn into a textile surface.

RIGHT: Wire comes in many forms and thicknesses and colours too. Lengths of wood dowel can be used as support for flimsy fabrics or cut up as beads. Waxed paper straws can be cut and decorated.

Wireform is available in a variety of weights and meshes. It can be easily cut with scissors or tin snips and bent and shaped as required. Other materials can be sewn to it or embedded into it.

Care must be taken when cutting wire, as small fragments have a habit of flying up into the air. Always wear safety glasses when carrying out this task. Ends of cut wire should be carefully finished to prevent them working their way through fabric and causing cuts and scratches. Bend the end back on to itself and then twist tightly with pliers.

Millinery wire is covered with a coating of fabric that renders it less slippery than ordinary wire. It can be used as a support and sewn into fabric.

PLASTICS

Plastics in the form of tubing, straws, bottles or packaging are all useful. More specific details will be given whenever it is used throughout the book.

CLAYS

Air-hardening clay and **Fimo** are both used for bead making. See chapter 6 for more on beads.

STIFFENING SOLUTIONS

PVA glue is well known among embroiderers as a vital accessory, whether used in the design process, to stabilize loose ends of thread or as a means of mounting finished work. But it is also possible to stiffen fabric by soaking it in a watered-down solution of PVA glue. The fabric can be manipulated into shape and, when dry, stitching may be added. It does change the surface of the fabric, leaving it with the feel and sometimes the look of plastic. This may be an important factor when choosing your method of forming your three-dimensional shape. If you are going to add stitch or more fabric after stiffening, the surface will be covered, but if the stiffening process is the final stage, you may want to consider whether or not a plastic finish is what you are aiming for and whether it is an appropriate finish for your subject. For me, this would be the last choice, as I would prefer to find an alternative method of supporting the fabric.

Starch is a long-time favourite for stiffening fabric, not for embroidery, but as a laundering process. Think of the heavily starched collars or table linen that were the norm for our grandmothers. However, either spray starch or the powdered versions provide a useful method of stiffening fine or flimsy fabrics.

Blind spray is normally used for stiffening fabric for blinds. It will give a firm finish to fabrics and will prevent edges fraying. Remember to protect yourself by using a mask when working with spray solutions.

Gesso is a substance that is used for priming canvases and for repairing the moulding on ornate picture frames. It can also be painted on to fabric to add strength and stiffness. It dries white, but can be painted afterwards. It is too hard to stitch into when dry.

Hot wax can be painted on to fabric before or after stitching to strengthen or add body to fabric or stitch. Working with a waxed thread, when binding elements together, adds firmness to the join and this can be further waxed when stitching is complete. Before you start, be sure that the waxy finish is appropriate to your subject.

Acrylic varnish that is water soluble is useful when making silk or viscose paper and can also be used for stiffening fabric.

Tools and equipment
CUTTING AND MANIPULATING EQUIPMENT

A separate pair of **scissors** for cutting paper and fabric is necessary, as cutting paper will quickly blunt the scissors that you use for fabric. **Shears** are recommended for thick fabrics. Use **tin snips** for metal and wire.

When working with wood, a **tenon saw** is necessary. A small **hobby drill** is useful to make holes in wood, with very tiny drill bits being available. An ordinary household drill can do the job just as well, although it is heavier to use.

A **craft knife**, **steel ruler** and **cutting mat** to protect surfaces will be needed to cut card, paper and plastic.

Pliers are essential for cutting and bending wire. They can be useful, too, when extra help is needed to pull a needle through thick fabric.

BELOW: Scissors of various kinds are essential together with a craft knife, steel ruler and cutting mat.

Small, round-nosed **jeweller's pliers** are useful when working with fine wires as they mark the wire as little as possible. **Flat-nose pliers** are also needed as they grip the wire better when twisting or manipulating wire, and wire nippers are required for cutting and trimming wire and wire mesh.

A **coiling gizmo** is used for winding wires. This simple tool can wind fine wires into small springs and is used for bead making.

A **cord winder** can be used to create decorative cords for coiling, couching and stitching. This is not an essential tool as cords can be hand twisted, but it does give a professional finish to cords and longer lengths can more easily be made.

HEAT TOOLS

A **soldering iron** is not only used for soldering metals together. In the context of embroidery it can be used to cut through man-made fabrics such as acrylic felt. Intricate edges in fine fabrics such as nylon can be cut with a soldering iron and fabrics that readily fray can be sealed when treated in this way. It will make holes in plastics and Perspex and can make interesting marks in wood.

A **hot air tool**, designed for hobby and craft use, can melt and distort fabrics and plastics. Some of these tools look like hairdryers, so they should be safely stored away when not in use, where they cannot be found by children or anyone not aware of their use.

Great care must be taken when using heat tools. Remember to follow the instructions and guidelines provided by the manufacturer. Protect yourself by wearing a suitable mask and your surroundings by using a heat-resistant mat or a ceramic tile, and making sure that you work in a tidy space away from clutter and other materials that could be damaged if in the way.

PROTECTING SURFACES

Protecting surfaces is important and a **heatproof mat** designed for use in soldering and available from DIY stores is essential. I also use a **kiln shelf**, which is designed to withstand very high temperatures. These can be bought from a ceramic supplier.

Baking parchment should be used with your domestic iron to protect its surface and that of the ironing board when working with Bondaweb (fusible webbing).

LEFT: Heat tools are used for cutting and melting.

ABOVE: A range of brushes will be needed to record information and making a variety of marks.

DESIGN

A sketchbook is necessary for recording ideas, together with a range of drawing pencils, pens, paints, crayons and coloured inks and brushes. It is the place where the germ of an idea may start, perhaps with a rough sketch of something seen and recorded at the time, and developed into something more concrete and definite at a later date.

DRAFTING MATERIALS

Grey board and **white ticket card** are both needed for trying out shapes and structures, together with masking tape to make temporary joins. Grey board is available in a variety of thicknesses and the thicker ones, although harder to cut, will make a very strong shape and could be seen as a permanent base on which to add your textile. Ticket card can be cut with scissors but a more accurate straight line is achieved with a craft knife and steel ruler. In practice, I utilize any kind of card that comes my way, especially if it is to be used for trying out ideas rather than for a finished model. So much packaging accompanies anything that we buy, so it is good to be able to reuse and recycle it whenever possible.

Cutting equipment includes a craft knife with spare blades, a steel ruler and a cutting mat to protect surfaces. The self-closing ones are useful as they have accurate grids marked on them, which help to keep verticals and horizontals at right angles to each other. Setsquares can help here too. Working with a craft knife requires great care and concentration to prevent accidents happening.

HB pencils are ideal for accurate drafting, as they will hold a sharp point when measuring and marking out.

Squared or **graph paper** is needed when working with geometrics. I prefer to count squares rather than measure off with a ruler as I find them easier to see. Isometric graph paper is useful too as it is good with equilateral triangles and hexagons.

Masking tape or **paper clips** are quick-and-easy solutions to making fast joins. Both can be removed to leave no mark.

DECORATION

A variety of paints may be needed, together with a range of brushes to apply it. These may be acrylic, emulsion or fabric paints. Dedicated brushes should be used for glue, wax and varnish, and the appropriate cleaning solution used. It is worth taking the trouble to look after brushes, as they are expensive to buy. If they are cleaned up and dried immediately they should last for a long time.

SUPPORTS AND FORMERS

When constructing with textiles, it is often necessary to have some method of support if the fabric of the piece is too flimsy or fragmented to support itself. The support may be built into the structure as an integral framework to the piece or it may be a temporary aid to help shape and form the fabric during construction. This method of support is withdrawn once the fabric is stable enough to hold up on its own.

When working with silk paper, handmade paper or fabric made by machine stitching on hot- or cold-water soluable film, many embroiderers are tempted to use a pudding basin as a former. This is not a good idea because a machine-made bowl usually has a turned foot at its base and will leave this manufactured stamp imprinted on your handcrafted shape unless steps are taken to block it out.

Polystyrene balls and other shapes are available in many sizes, with larger ones divided into two halves. Fabric can be pinned into the surface while work is in progress. Layers of tissue paper can be pasted over them without being permanently stuck to the surface.

Blocks of styrofoam are used to create a supporting form. It can be cut, sawn, sanded, drilled and modelled, so is very useful when a specific shape or non-standard, one-off shape is required.

LEFT: A collection of polystyrene balls and styrofoam provides good support for three-dimensional work.

RIGHT: Thick rolls of card can be built into the work as a permanent support.

Cane from basket makers' suppliers or hobby shops can be woven and manipulated to form a framework for further embellishment with fabrics and stitching. It is a flexible material that can be adapted to many situations.

Wooden hat blocks are normally used only for steaming felt for hats, but they are also useful as a former for vessels and a support for curved surfaces. They can withstand some heat and fabric can be pinned or stuck to the surface with masking tape.

Card rolls of various kinds, from kitchen paper to carpet rolls, are very helpful in supporting work in progress. Office suppliers sell card rolls for storing and sending documents through the post, but your local recycling centre may have some that will cost you nothing.

Chapter 3
Constructing with flat pieces

In this chapter, I consider repetition of shape in geometric form and in the form of slices of shape, as well as flat shapes that enclose space. Many exciting forms can be created by joining together flat pieces of stiffened fabric. These may be either regular geometric shapes or shapes that are drawn without the constraint of geometry. Freely drawn flat shapes may be random, asymmetric or organic in style, with edges being straight or curved, crisp, ragged or shaped. Alternatively, flat, geometric planes may be repeated as cross-sections or slices of form, rather than having their edges joined to enclose space.

If enclosed space is the aim, there is plenty of scope to contrast inside and outside surfaces with colour, texture, pattern or tone. Inspiration for this is endless within the natural world. The surfaces of flower petals and leaves often have contrasting inner and outer colour or texture. Seedpods and fruits may have a hard outside shell but can be soft inside. They may be subdivided into sections or compartments, such as with oranges and grapefruits. A walnut has a tough, thick membrane that fits snugly round the nut inside.

Repetition of a unit of design can produce rhythm and harmony. Most pattern is composed of repetition. When scaled down it can produce a complex texture to a surface. Repetition may be considered in a number of different ways: repeating shape; repeating the size or scale of a shape; repeating units of colour or texture, the direction of a shape or element within a form. Repeats can give a sense of order.

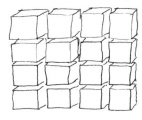 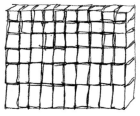 

LEFT: Cubes can be stacked together to form a structure. The unit size of the cube can be varied to give a different look to the piece.

Geometrics

When flattened, all geometric forms become networks, which are repeating, intersecting lines that underpin all repeat pattern. Sometimes the lines become part of the pattern but often they remain just as a guide for placing motifs within a given space. The spaces between net lines are shapes that will interlock or connect with others within the same network. We generally think of pattern as being flat, or relatively so, but if geometric shapes are repeated as forms, three-dimensional pattern can be created.

When unit forms are repeated exactly the arrangement can be rather boring, but if they are graduated in size or placement the result is a much more interesting structure.

Variations:
- Combine large units with small ones or squares with oblongs.
- They can be randomly placed or staggered.

BELOW: Metal thread layers constructed from repeated frames cut from Pelform and covered with bonded fabric. The frames forming the outside edge have been decorated with metal-thread machine stitching, cords, cut purl and beading. The inside panels were worked on dissolvable fabric, with areas melted away using a soldering iron, and set between the outer panels. The frames have been spaced using beads. (Christine Smith)

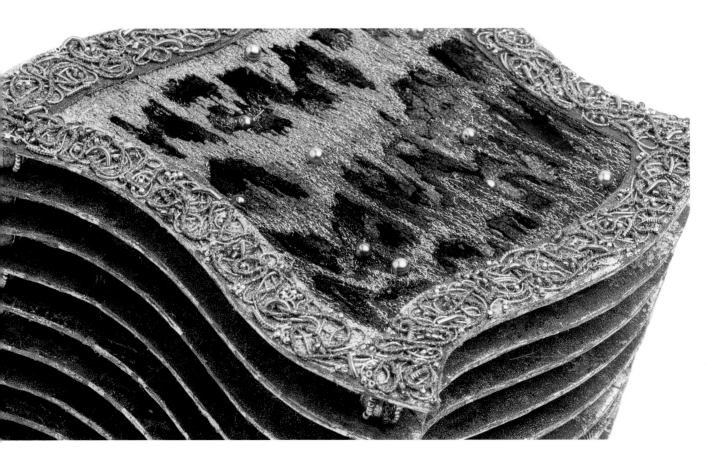

- Straight edges can be made to curve.
- Vary the depth of the unit.
- Cut away the front plane to create a cell and place another shape within.
- The shape within could extend beyond the basic cell.

SQUARES AND RECTANGLES

A square or rectangular net can be arranged in a number of ways that will fold up to become an enclosed box. Six units are needed to do this, four for the sides and one each for top and bottom. Whatever the size of the square, it will always look balanced and stable because the dimensions of height and width and depth are equal. It would be possible, however, to vary the measurements of

LEFT: A square box, set on a plinth. A raised circle has been added to extend the top and sides. Thick card and wadding have been used to pad the circles.

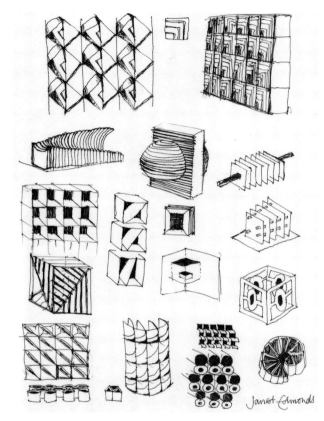

ABOVE: Cubes of varying sizes are stacked together to make a three-dimensional pattern. Some of the cubes are open on one side to form a cell. The colour or texture of the inside of the cell can be different to the outside to add further interest.

RIGHT: Some ideas that demonstrate how shapes can be repeated to form larger structures.

RIGHT: Squares within squares and cubic modules create exciting possibilities for three-dimensional pattern. These squares are joined with a small link to give more space between the shapes.

BELOW: A small square is suspended within a larger one.

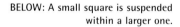

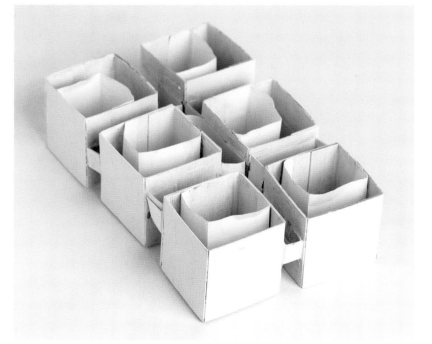

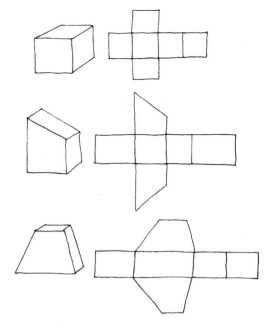

the unit. Instead of having planes at right angles to each other, as in a standard regular cube, the angles could be changed to alter the look of the cube. Any of these shapes could form the basis of a simple box.

Interest could be added to a simple square or rectangular box by creating a raised surface pattern on some or all of the units. For the purposes of stability, it would need to sit on a flat plane or have four feet to stand on, but the remaining five planes could be decorated. The centres of each square, for example, could be raised to a point, or a further shape could be added to each section. Alternatively, another, smaller shape could be set into the basic square, creating a raised centre with a border around it. Instead of adding dimension to the surface, another idea would be to cut some of the surface away so that it is possible to look through the form and see planes beyond.

ABOVE: All three-dimensional, geometric shapes open out to form a flat net. These shapes can be plotted on graph paper to ensure that the vertical and horizontal edges are at right angles to each other.

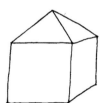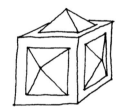

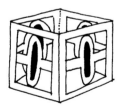

ABOVE (TOP): Cube with an added raised shape.

ABOVE: Spaces can be cut out of the sides of a cube to form an open pattern.

LEFT: The sides of this square box have been cut so that it is possible to see through the shape. In this case, consideration should be give to both the inside and outside surfaces.

ABOVE AND RIGHT: A small gift box is constructed from six squares linked together in pairs. When the cord is drawn up the squares form a box. A bead holds the box closed.

BELOW: Diagram showing the layout of the gift box.

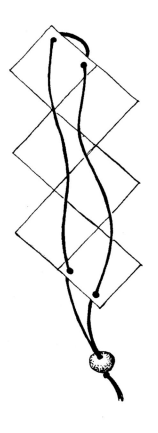

Gift box

To make a small gift box like the one pictured above:

1 Arrange six squares in pairs, offsetting each row so that the squares are staggered.

2 Cut six squares out of thick card 50mm (2in) square.

3 Cut two pattern shapes from craft weight Vilene as shown. The squares are 55mm (2⅛in) square.

4 Bond silk fabric to each one and trim it.

5 Decorate at this stage if you wish.

6 Put Vilene sides together and machine stitch along the intersections between the squares.

7 Using a satin stitch, stitch over the edges to close them, slipping the card into each section as you go.

8 Pierce holes at the positions marked.

9 Thread a machine cord through the holes and add a bead by threading the ends of the cord through it and knotting the ends together. Whip the raw ends to neaten.

10 Pull the bead up along the cord to close the shape.

Repeats of cubed squares or rectangles can be combined to create dimensional pattern. By joining them together in different ways, a variety of patterns may be achieved. Three flat squares joined edge to edge will give an equilateral triangle, which can then be treated as a unit shape and repeated. In the example, the ends of the form are open, but it would be possible to add a further plane to close the end or add one at both ends.

Dimensional pattern
This is how to make a dimensional pattern.

Requirements:
- Coloured Vilene (this could be decorated with stitching or patterned with machine embroidery)
- Cutting equipment
- Sewing machine and threads
- Hand-sewing equipment

1 Cut 18 small rectangles, 45mm x 30mm (1¾ x 1⅛in) from Vilene.

2 Seam them together by matching two edges and machine stitch these together using a narrow zigzag. Remember to reverse the stitching each end of the seam to secure the zigzag.

3 Join a third rectangle to complete one triangle.

4 Join the other 15 rectangles together in the same way.

5 With hand stitch sew two seams together and join two triangles together.

RIGHT: This box is constructed from three oblong segments joined together to form six cells. Each section has been stitched with machine embroidery, worked on cold-water-dissolvable film, onto a fine wire frame. The surface of the stitching has been painted with fabric stiffener to add strength to the surface.

BELOW: Three oblongs are seamed together make a hollow triangle. This process can be repeated to form a three-dimensional pattern.

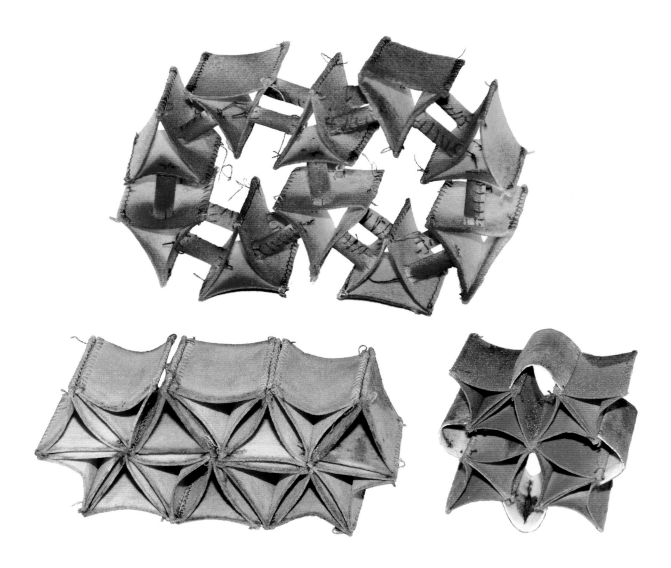

6 Continue joining in pairs.

7 Now join pairs together until you have a circle of triangles, which, if repeated, will create further circles. It can be extended in any direction for a larger form.

If several cubes, open on one plane, are joined together, a network of compartments is formed. Inside the enclosed space further shapes or divisions can be placed, resulting in a more complex form.

ABOVE: Triangular samples show the patterns that can be made when the shapes are arranged in different ways.

ABOVE: A set of small, equilateral triangles are fitted together and contained by a larger one.

RIGHT: Equilateral triangles are combined to create larger, more complex forms.

TRIANGLES

Equilateral triangles offer lots of opportunity to create shape and form. Because they tessellate, they create circles when six are placed together. Five joined together make a cup form and six give an undulating cup shape.

Five small, three-dimensional triangles fit exactly into one larger one. When triangles are repeated, a cellular structure is formed. This idea could be adapted for making boxes with lids and bases added to complete the shape.

Triangles with two sides equal and one smaller, create wedges, which in turn make circles. Top and bottom edges need not be straight but could be varied depending on how the structure is to stand.

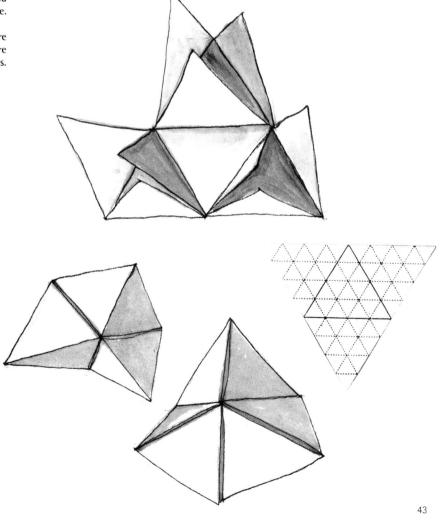

FAR LEFT: Drawing of an Aboriginal *Pukumani* burial post from Arnhem Land in Australia.

LEFT: Aboriginal burial posts have inspired a mock-up for a totem, reflecting shape and surface patterns.

ABOVE: Drawings that were developed while looking at models of Aztec temples. These sketches could be developed into finished pieces built on to a basic cylinder shape.

ABOVE CENTRE AND RIGHT: Patterns developed from Aboriginal *Pukumani* burial posts. The patterns were printed as collagraphs and were combined with monoprints on tissue paper. These were cut up and torn, and applied to the surface to add texture.

CYLINDERS

Cardboard tubes left behind from kitchen rolls are a useful ready resource when circles or cylinders are needed. Pile them up randomly or thread one through another. Chop them up and stand them close together for a cellular effect. Vary the height or cut into the surface or edges. Further shapes can be added along the length or they could be slotted together.

If you are unable to find a ready-made cylinder to adapt, it is possible to construct one of the height and diameter that you want. Thick card will crack if it is bent too sharply so to avoid this paint one side with water to dampen. Carefully bend around a bottle or jar of the right size and secure with elastic bands and leave to dry. If a small diameter is needed, you may have to repeat the process and gradually tighten the curve of the card in stages until the required size is reached.

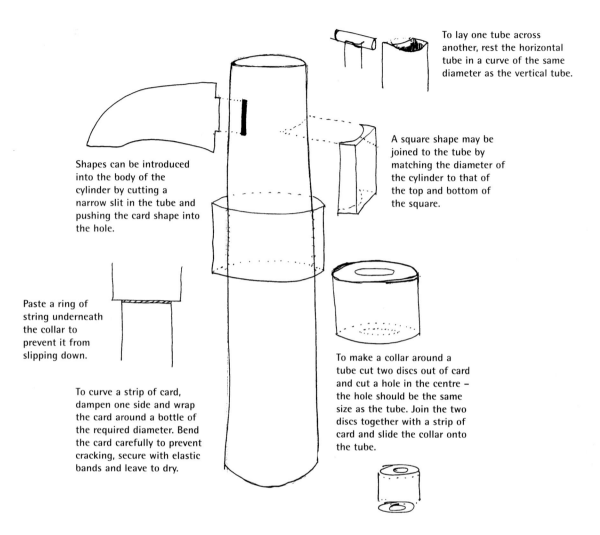

To lay one tube across another, rest the horizontal tube in a curve of the same diameter as the vertical tube.

Shapes can be introduced into the body of the cylinder by cutting a narrow slit in the tube and pushing the card shape into the hole.

A square shape may be joined to the tube by matching the diameter of the cylinder to that of the top and bottom of the square.

Paste a ring of string underneath the collar to prevent it from slipping down.

To curve a strip of card, dampen one side and wrap the card around a bottle of the required diameter. Bend the card carefully to prevent cracking, secure with elastic bands and leave to dry.

To make a collar around a tube cut two discs out of card and cut a hole in the centre – the hole should be the same size as the tube. Join the two discs together with a strip of card and slide the collar onto the tube.

Covering a curved surface is tricky. Ideally the fabric should be cut on the cross so that there is a degree of give as the fabric is stretched around the cylinder. This should avoid wrinkles in the fabric and it is possible to achieve a snug fit. In practice, it is likely that the fabric will be embellished with stitch, thus inhibiting the stretch of the fabric. In this case, provided the fabric to be attached is backed with another, it may be necessary to stick the textile to the card using good quality PVA glue, such as that used for gluing wood. Alternatively, attach the embroidery to the card with Bondaweb while it is still flat and curl it into a cylinder afterwards.

A cylinder could also serve as a former while work is in progress or it could be covered with fabric and remain as an integral part of the piece.

FACING PAGE
LEFT: A vessel is constructed from layers of fabric. Blue cotton fabric is bonded with orange satin material and the circles decrease in size as the height rises. They are threaded onto a core of coloured Vilene.

RIGHT: Double-sided fabric is layered using threading techniques.

STRIPS AND SLICES

Many exciting ideas can be developed from linear sources. Buildings, railings, fences and electric pylons all have the common characteristic of strips. They can be found in the natural world too. Mushroom gills, markings on shells, veining on leaves and stems, and the characteristic ridges of ploughed fields are all familiar examples of the repeated line.

Pieces of stiffened fabric placed close together with a small spacer between each layer or placed one on top of another will give a ridged effect that can be varied by using either a cut edge, a torn edge or a stitched one.

Lengths of firm fabric piled layer on layer can be shaped or curved to give a sculptural look. Randomly cut circles piled up could form cylinders or bowls.

Slices of stiffened fabric, layer upon layer, can create rich effects when the surface is decorated with machine stitch. The outside shape may be regular and geometric or irregular and organic in style. Try cutting the middle out of the slice of fabric and work stitching across the space. When several layers are set together, a three-dimensional pattern is formed, and it is possible to look through and into the structure.

Strips of fabric that have been stiffened by bonding two layers together can be arranged in a variety of ways. Stitch them to a backing and try these ideas.

Variations:
- Make them into a cylinder.
- Bond different coloured fabrics together.
- Combine a plain-coloured fabric with a machine-stitched one.
- Alternate one texture with another texture or one colour with another colour.
- Vary the shape of the edges of the strip.
- Insert strips into a length of fabric by slashing through the fabric and passing the edges of the strip through. Then stitch to hold.

ABOVE: The shape that forms this piece was developed from wrought-iron decoration on the roof of a glasshouse at Kew Gardens, London. The form was based on the idea of slate tiles slotted together, found on a water feature in the gardens. Satin backed with calico is supported by craft-weight Vilene and the shapes are spaced with wrapped felt and wired to provide some flexibility to the whole. (Marian Spencer)

ABOVE: A sample of layered, bonded fabric. One end of the shape is joined to a strip of fabric making the piece very flexible. Wonderful effects are created as the fabric moves.

RIGHT: Thread is wrapped around wire frames and machine embroidery is worked onto the surface. Several frames are layered together with tiny, Vilene shapes creating space between them. It is possible to look through and into the complex structure.

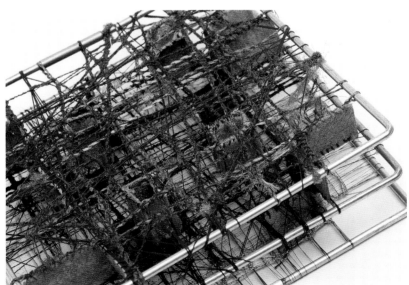

Free form

Shapes developed from organic sources can be pieced together to create vessels.

Inspiration is found in the natural world by looking at seed pods and plant forms. The variety of forms and structures is endless but there are a few favourites. The ever-popular poppy seed head is a wonderful shape with a lid supported on pillars and, when disintegrated by wind and weather, the underlying structure can be seen. The seed case of the henbane has a five-pointed top edge with delicate veining like cutwork. This form is the protection for a tiny rounded inner vessel with a close-fitting lid. I have used this seed case as inspiration for vessels a number of times as it is such a satisfying shape.

FACING PAGE
TOP LEFT: A torn paper drawing, developed from a henbane seed pod, would be ideal for making cutwork designs. The design could be applied to squares or oblongs.

TOP RIGHT: Samples showing how each segment is constructed. Brown paper is bonded to a heavyweight Vilene shape. The paper is then dampened and manipulated to distress the surface and texture is added with machine stitching.

BELOW: These cutwork vessels were made by repeating each segment five times and seaming them together. Inspiration came from seed pods, which often have five segments.

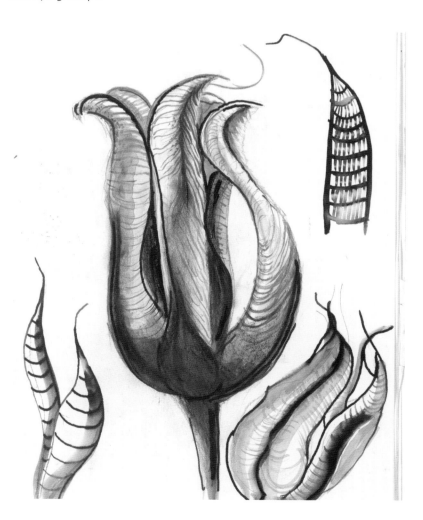

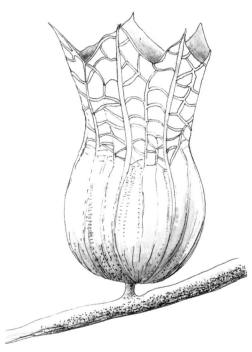

ABOVE: Henbane seed pod.

LEFT: This drawing of *Aquilegia vulgaris* would be ideal for a free-form, repeated shape, using either the whole or individual segments.

LEFT: A vessel formed by repeating the same shape many times. The calico shapes are threaded onto a strong linen thread and small fabric beads are used to create space between each piece of fabric.

BELOW: A paper sample showing repeated triangles, each one curved and held in place with a rod of plastic.

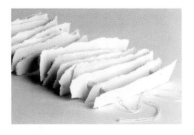

ABOVE: Strips are torn from heavy, handmade paper and threaded with strong thread. Paper shapes are added to form a space between each layer, creating a flexible element that can be manipulated into a free-form structure.

The unit shapes are best developed in paper or card first to determine the curve of the edges. Alterations are easily and quickly made until the required curve is achieved. A shallow curve on an edge will create a reasonably rounded form when several panels are seamed together, but it is worth taking the trouble to experiment to develop the right shape and to work out how many pieces will be needed to make up the whole. Make temporary joins using masking tape as they are easily taken apart if adjustments are needed.

Segmented shapes are cut out in fabric and worked flat, supported to stiffen as necessary with Vilene or felt, and decorated with colour and stitch. All edges are neatened before seaming together. To do this, place a fine cord alongside the edge and attach with a free machine zigzag stitch. Lengthen the stitch so that you do not have a satin stitch that would give a very obvious look to the edge. If you match the colour, the cord and the stitching will blend into the piece without drawing attention to themselves.

Further shaping is achieved by cutting an open dart. More detail on using darts can be found in chapter 5 (Manipulative techniques). The edges of the dart are neatened as described earlier. The two edges are brought together and stitched by hand with a matching thread. Take the needle through the thickness of the fabric so that very little thread shows.

Combining shapes can result in exciting structures, especially if angular ones are grouped with curvilinear ones.

Experiment with repeating shapes and combining by threading them on to either a flexible medium such as thick thread, cord or wire as in a mobile, or with a rigid one, which could be a fine tube, such as a drinking straw, plastic tubing or a wooden stick. A barbeque or lolly stick could be used for this or a length of dowel. All these could be painted or wrapped with fabric or thread.

Ideas:
- Flat strips could be curved and held with a rigid element thus contrasting a curve with a straight.
- A ring of thick material pierced with a rigid strip.
- Combinations of threaded shapes – squares with tubes – triangles with tubes – triangles with circles.

Chapter 4
Continuous lengths

Coiling

Coiling is a long-established basketry process in which the material that forms the **foundation** is stitched together with a flexible element called the **binder**. Most cultures have made and used coiled baskets for centuries, and in many areas of the world techniques are highly sophisticated with complex patterns finely worked in a variety of materials.

Working with a continuous length of fibre, the structure of the form is created by stitching over a core and securing the coils together. The coiling begins at the centre of the base of a form and spirals round and round, finishing at the rim with further lengths grafted in to maintain the length of the foundation. There are many decorative methods of stitching the foundation and almost any shape can be created as the work progresses. Alternatively, it may be stitched invisibly through the centre of the core. It is a very flexible technique but a slow process. The finer the foundation, the thinner the walls of the form will be and the slower the process.

THE FOUNDATION
The foundation can be made from lengths of torn fabric, bundles of thread, machine-made cords, wire, stitched or wrapped with thread, cane (as in traditional baskets), plastic tubing or indeed anything that has a length to it. There are some wonderful textured yarns on the market that are difficult to stitch with but ideal to use either as the foundation for coiling, or for the wrapping.

WRAPPING
Decoration may be added to the foundation in the form of stitching, as in machine-made cords, but wrapping with another thread can give an interesting effect and is a good way of blending colour or adding in texture. If the foundation is to be stitched invisibly, the wrapping can look like a stitched mark on the surface.

RIGHT: A continuous length of wrapped fabric was sewn together to form small, hollow pockets. Lots of these were stitched together to make the vessel.

Fabric can be wrapped with either thread or wire or, conversely, thread or wire can be wrapped with fabric. Extra decorative elements can be added in as wrapping progresses, such as beads, sequins, tufts of fabric or thread, pompons, small tassels, pieces of wood or small sticks. Care should be taken to make sure that these additions are not too bulky as the binding process could be frustrating, with the wrapping thread catching on the additions with every stitch.

Wrapping fabric with thread

Method:

1 Begin by tearing a length of fabric and choosing a thread that is firm but not too fine. Once you have a feel for the action and tension required to wrap a length of fabric, you can progress to 'trickier' threads.

2 Lay about 30mm (11/8in) of the wrapping thread along the end of the fabric bundle and begin wrapping it firmly over the fabric and the laid thread. This traps the end of the wrapping thread and prevents it from unravelling. Hold the fabric that you are wrapping close to where the binding is taking place and keep the binding quite close together, about 2 or 3mm apart. If your binding is too spaced out the wrapping will be floppy and loose but when it is right it takes on a wiry quality and is quite stiff.

3 To finish off, tie the end of the wrapping thread with an overhand knot to secure.

It is easier to work a series of short lengths of foundation and graft them together as the stitching progresses, since these are more comfortable to make. The longer the foundation, the more difficult

ABOVE: Samples of wrapping, some with beads and sequins added.

BELOW: Lay the wrapping thread along the fabric to be wrapped. Hold the fabric bundle between finger and thumb and start to wrap the thread around it firmly. When you get to the end, loop the thread through the last wrap and pull to tighten.

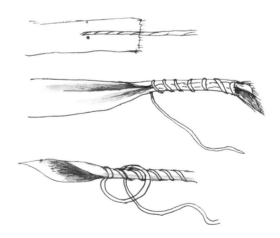

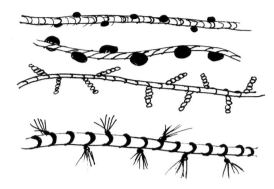

the wrapping because the thread will get into a muddle and you will have to keep unscrambling it. I work with lengths of about 30–35cm (12–14in) of foundation and fairly short lengths of wrapping thread.

Variations:
- Try hand wrapping a machine-made cord.
- Thread beads on to the wrapping thread before starting to wrap. Place a bead at intervals as you bind the foundation.
- Wrap a fabric foundation with fine coloured wire, the type used for jewellery.
- Wrap with a contrast thread, such as black on white; pairs of complementary colours, red and green, blue and orange, purple and yellow.
- Wrap several times to blend colour.
- As wrapping progresses, include bands of contrasting-coloured fabric around the foundation before wrapping with a matching thread.

ABOVE: Ideas for decorating wrapped cords.

RIGHT: A small pot is woven using machine cords as a weft. Hand-wrapped cotton cords are used as the warp.

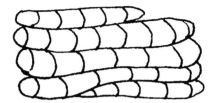

LEFT: Wind the wrapped fabric into a coil and secure with stitching. This is a good method to begin to form a shape.

RIGHT: Detail of a wrapped vessel.

CONSTRUCTION

Coiling as a method of construction is very simple. Wrapped lengths are bound together in a continuous coil, starting at the centre of the base, either by stitching through the centre of the foundation (invisible) or by further binding over the foundation, which gives decoration in the form of another mark on the surface.

Invisible method

Use a strong thread for the invisible method. Buttonhole thread, linen or cotton, crochet cotton or any thread marked 'extra strong' will be suitable. The colour is immaterial, as it is not going to show. You will need a strong sharp needle with a suitably sized eye to take the thread. You may need a small pair of pliers to push the needle in and out depending on how tightly you have wrapped your foundation. Begin by attaching your sewing thread to one end of the foundation. Curl the end into itself to start the coiling action and fasten with a stitch taken through the thickness of the foundation. Continue curling the foundation and stitching it in place as you go.

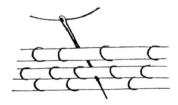

ABOVE: Diagram demonstrating how to use the invisible method.

Wrapped method

The thread for the wrapped method does not have to be quite so strong as it is not going to be passed through fabric, but it should not be so soft that it breaks when you pull it firmly to tension the wrapping. You will need a blunt needle or a bodkin, depending on your choice of thread. The thread may be textured or have a dimension to it, such as narrow ribbon or flat braid. The foundation does not have to be wrapped first but it could be, as this is a good method of creating a blend of colour.

First attach the thread to the end of the foundation. You may need to do this with a finer needle and sewing cotton. Curl the end of the foundation into itself as before, but this time you are going to fasten coils together by passing the binding thread around the foundation in a wrapping action. As you progress, take the thread in a figure of eight around two coils. The end result with this method tends to be rather softer than the invisible method, so choose the technique that gives you the feel that you want.

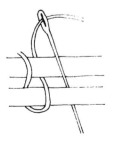

ABOVE: Diagram showing the figure-of-eight technique.

SHAPING

Almost any shape may be formed using coiling, although edges and corners will be rounded. The coils may be manipulated to leave holes and spaces, and bowl constructions may move in and out to form enclosed shapes or flared-out rims. It is a very flexible medium enabling the coils to fold back on themselves or spiral in or out to create more complex forms. To change direction, place the foundation slightly to one side or the other of the previous row, tipping it inwards or outwards, gently easing the shape to decrease or increase in size.

Flat pieces of fabric can be made with this technique and then joined together to create form as discussed in chapter 3. Shapes may be formed by manipulating coiled planes in almost any direction and stitching them together where necessary.

Another method of shaping is to use a former. Commercially available polystyrene shapes are useful for this as the wrappings can be pinned in place to support the shape while stitching is progressing. Alternatively, card rolls or any other preformed shape may be utilized, either as a temporary support or covered with wrapped lengths if a permanent rigid support is needed.

ABOVE: A torn-paper drawing was the inspiration for this wrapped fabric. Lengths of wrapping are joined as required to make a particular shape.

LEFT: A polystyrene shape supports a number of hand-stitched machine cords. The patterns on the surface are stitched with gold metallic thread.

RIGHT: Hand-wrapped fabric lengths are machine-stitched to a felt backing.

FINISHING

When your form has grown to the desired size and shape you will need to taper the foundation to smooth and blend off the rim. This is easier with the first, invisible method described above, as the thread is passing through the foundation, although you may need to cut some of the thickness away. Similarly with the wrapped method, pare away some of the thickness of the foundation and fasten the end with a fine needle and sewing cotton to match. A stiletto is a useful tool to help separate coils to enable ends to be tucked in to neaten.

Variations:

- Try coiling bundles of foundation elements together, perhaps only stitching them together at intervals.
- Experiment with stitch patterns when wrapping coils together.
- Add other decorative elements while forming the shape. Stitch in feathers, small shells, rolls of paper, bundles of thread or beads.
- Create flat shapes and join them together or combine them with other techniques.
- Machine stitch wrappings on to a backing of felt using a narrow zigzag.

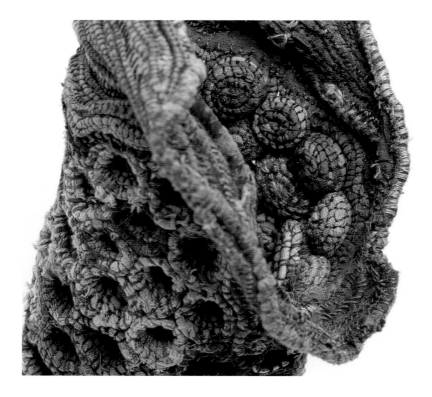

LEFT: The inside of the vessel has a raised surface.

ABOVE: A combination of natural and man-made materials inspired this coiled vessel. A wire and plastic core is wrapped with cotton fabrics and stitched with thread. The binding has been further embellished with coloured, plastic parcel tape and beads. (Felicity Clarke)

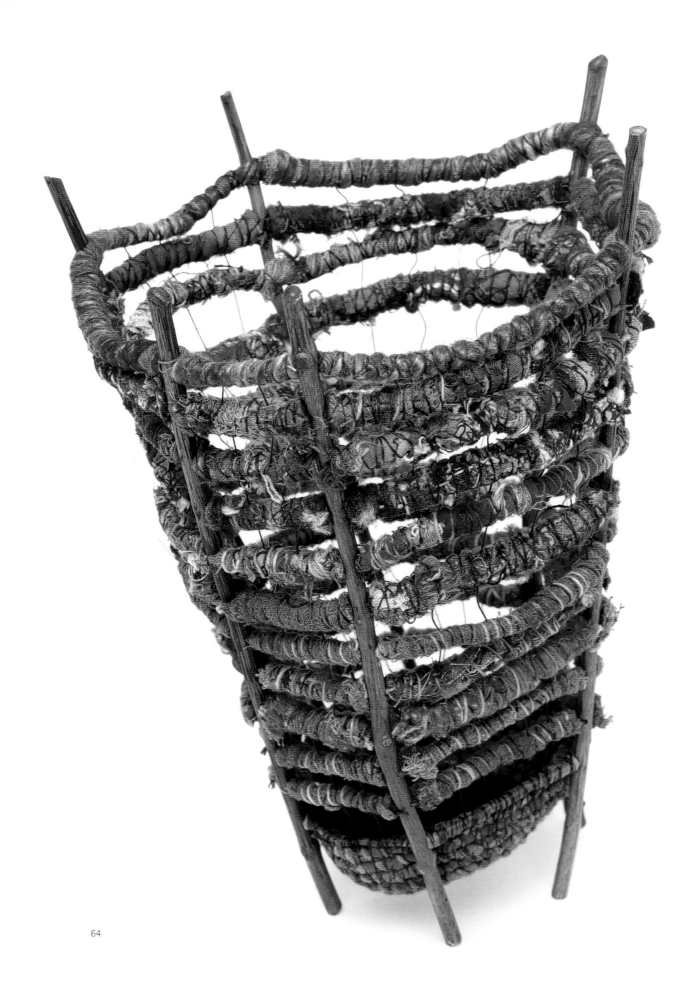

Free-form building with continuous lengths

Any material that is continuous in length and is flexible but not too floppy can be utilized for creating in three dimensions, whether it is paper in the form of string or cut lengths stuck or joined together. There are various thicknesses of paper string, from fine to chunky or twisted, such as the type used for floristry. Some plant material can be cut fresh and used while green and flexible. I have successfully worked with lengths of privet and grape vine, but hazel and all varieties of cane, as used by basket makers, are particularly good choices.

Wire can be used for this free-form method too. Fine wire is suitable if small, delicate shapes are required or you can scale up for larger shapes and use thick copper wire or millinery wire. Electrical wires come already coloured as they are encased in a plastic insulating material, but if colour or decoration is needed at the outset before constructing, paper is easily dyed or painted, and wire can either be wrapped or machined over. This needs some care, as the needle will break if it hits the wire as you are stitching. Set your machine up with a zigzag stitch that is wide enough to just cover the wire. If it is too tight around the wire the needle is much more likely to hit it. Proceed carefully and watch it all the time as wire can bounce around and it is easy to go off course.

Method:
Begin by winding the material around into curls and curves. Anchor the points where two lengths cross each other either with masking tape for a temporary join or by tying with string or binding with fine wire. This gives a basic shape that can be manipulated as the winding progresses. Further lengths can then be worked into the framework by weaving in and out, filling in spaces as required.

It is a bit fiddly to get started but the process becomes easier to manage once you have a few wraps and overlaps in place, and these are fixed. The joins can be removed at a later stage when the form is more stable or they could be left in as a decorative element. I always marvel at how birds build their nests when I am working in this way. They do it all with just a beak and not a scrap of masking tape to assist.

LEFT: Lengths of wrapped fabric are threaded through vertical wooden supports. A coiled shape fills the base.

BELOW: To build a free-form object with a continuous length, wind it around a shape to support it, in this case a card tube. Where one length crosses another, tie, bind or sew them together to anchor them in place.

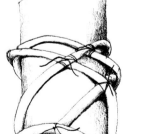

Variations:

- Try combining materials. Make a basic form out of wire and fill in with paper string or combine plant material with wire.
- Leave holes and spaces.
- Dip the form into paper pulp or pour the pulp over if the shape is a large one.
- Fit one shape inside another.
- Open out the weaving to form a bowl or close it in to create a bottle shape.
- Join several small shapes together to make a larger, more complex form.

LEFT: A detail of the nest. The surface was enhanced by pouring paper pulp over the nest, then adding extra pieces of newsprint.

ABOVE: A long length of vine cut
from the garden was woven into a
nest shape. Further strands of vine
were woven in until a firm structure
was formed.

LEFT: A card former was wrapped in silk string and painted with fabric stiffener. The piece was wrapped again with fine, coloured wires and decorated with added beads. A machine-stitched rim was sewn to the top edge.

DECORATION

When your basic form is complete you may wish to decorate it. There are many ways to do this and as embroiderers we have a wealth of methods to choose from. What method you choose may depend on what use or setting you plan for your form. If it is to be purely decorative, then anything goes, but if there is an element of function, consideration must be given to practicalities and this may limit choice. Decide whether or not you want to see inside and outside space, in which case you will need to leave some of the spaces open.

If you didn't use colour at the outset you could colour it at this stage by dyeing or painting as suggested earlier or the colour could come from the decoration that is applied to the structure.

Variations:

- Suspend beads, cloth or stitch into the spaces. The beads could be tiny purchased beads or ones you have made yourself. See chapter 6 for ideas. The cloth may be dyed, manipulated or stitched, or perhaps made on the machine using a dissolvable support. For stitching try woven wheels suspended into spaces or insertion stitches worked across holes.
- Tie thread, wires or fabric strips to the shape or wrap parts of it.
- Sew beads on to the surface. These could be paper beads if you have used paper for the weave or beads made from wire if you have used wire to make your shape.
- If you have dipped the form into paper pulp, this could be painted or dyed.

Chapter 5
Manipulated methods

There are many manipulative techniques that distort and texture the surface of fabric. This chapter explores some methods of treating fabric that result in not only changing the surface but also the structure of fabric, with the intention of making it distort and contort and curve in ways that can be exploited to create form.

Useful techniques might include gathering, making tucks, pleats or darts normally used in dressmaking, together with folding and knotting. Piecing and patching manipulated fabrics can result in exciting shapes that can be adapted for all manner of three-dimensional items, while traditional knitting and weaving techniques seen in this context can also inspire dimensional form.

Felt and paper, particularly if you make them yourself, open up lots of possibilities for forming and building, and ideas will be given on how they may be used. However, space will not be given here to the methods of making felt and paper, as there are many excellent publications that specialize in these techniques.

RIGHT: A felt vessel is manipulated with tucks, added cords and hand stitching.

BELOW: Drawings of driftwood can often suggest shapes for vessels, bags or boxes. These tiny pieces of wood have been worn smooth by the action of the sea and the exposed growth rings provide ideas for gathers, or tucks and pleats.

Fabrics

Some fabrics are suitable for specific processes and effects, and the various types that are available are too numerous to list here. However, some of the more versatile fabrics deserve a mention.

- **Calico** or **cotton sheeting** is endlessly useful. Calico is a robust fabric and comes in a variety of weights from fine to heavy furnishing. It is easily dyed or coloured and is relatively cheap. It is possible to achieve a good crease and cut edges will fray to give a soft effect but will not shred. The surface is matt and some types have a fleck in the weave. A bolt of calico would definitely come with me to my desert island! Cotton sheeting also dyes well and is readily found in fabric shops.
- **Scrim** is a fine, loosely woven fabric that is soft, gathers well and is ideal for layering and combining with other fabrics. The type used by plasterers, whether fine and narrow or coarse and narrow, is indispensable for binding, weaving or layering.

BELOW: A spiral form is constructed in manipulated sinemay, based on the golden section ratio. The fabric was soaked for a few seconds in warm water to make it pliable and then shaped on a paper-mâché base. Once dry, the material holds its shape, and is dyed and decorated with hand and machine stitch. (Diana Robertson)

RIGHT: Tissue paper moulded over a polystyrene ball provides the foundation for this delicate bowl. The inside has been embellished with pieces of paper straw that have been cut and waxed.

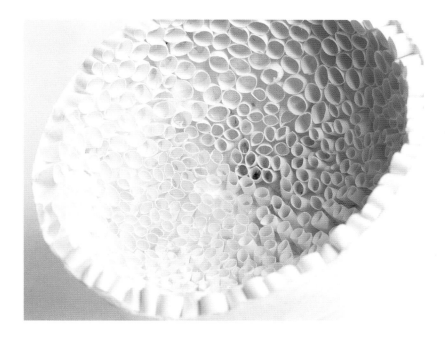

- **Hessian**, with its loose weave, is rough and coarse. It is readily distressed by pulling threads apart to make holes, and cut ends are tufty and hairy.
- **Organdie** is a light, delicate fabric giving crisp edges to folds and tucks. Its soft, transparent quality is good for tonal effects and layering.
- **Organza**, whether it is silk or man-made, is similarly light and transparent to organdie, but it has more drape, giving a softer effect.
- **Felt**, whether commercial or hand-made, is ideal for cutting and manipulating, as it is non-woven. Clean, non-fray edges when cut can be an advantage. It has a soft, matt, woolly surface and the acrylic type can be distorted with heat.
- **Sinemay** has an open weave and is made from stiff fibres. It is commonly used for millinery purposes as it can be wetted and moulded.
- **Tissue paper**, layered using PVA glue, over a polystyrene shape, is a good method of making bowls and vessels. Several layers will be needed before the required thickness is achieved. Fragments of textile or stitching can be added as layers build up. Some of the layers could be fine builders, such as scrim or fine cotton, as this adds texture and strength to the wall of the vessel and can give more of a textile feel to the piece. It is still possible to stitch into the surface to add decoration after construction is complete.

• **Man-made fabrics** that melt or distort under heat are worth experimenting with too as their properties of curling can be controlled or manipulated to create form. Caution is needed when working with these types of fabric and applying heat as some of them can flare suddenly or give off dangerous fumes. Make sure that you know what you are working with and conduct a test first under safe conditions with a small sample to familiarize yourself with the effects. Be sure to take proper precautions. Wear a mask and work in a well-ventilated room.

Manipulative techniques

GATHERING

When fabric is gathered using an evenly placed running stitch, line-by-line, small, regular folds that lie side-by-side result.

The fabric is reduced in length by one-third or more so this needs to be taken into account when preparing fabric ready for use. This method will give very simple cylindrical shapes. With large pieces of fabric the effects can be very dramatic.

BELOW LEFT: A sample of paper that has been painted and gathered.

BELOW: Two samples of gathering showing how different effects can be created by using evenly placed gathering stitches and randomly placed gathers.

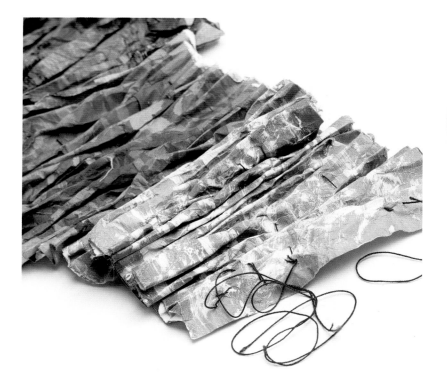

RIGHT: Table lamp with shade made from panels of dyed, painted and manipulated silk noil, combined with dyed, bonded silk chiffon, hand stitched with copper wire. (Barbara Robinson)

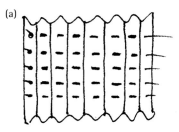
(a)

If, however, the gathers are stitched unevenly, with stitches that vary in length and spacing, it is possible to achieve curves with undulating surfaces. Fabric can be squashed and reduced in bulk, allowing form to emerge when the expansion and contraction of the fullness of the fabric is controlled.

By stitching in circles or squares, lumps, bumps and small raised areas are achieved. Pattern can form when the circles, squares or other shapes are stitched regularly.

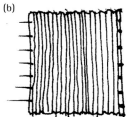
(b)

Gathers can be pulled tightly so that no stitching shows or fabric fullness can be eased out to expose the gathering thread. This gives a decorative opportunity as the thread could be a contrasting colour or variegated with the colour emerging and disappearing where the gathers open out or close up. Beads or surface additions could be threaded on to the gathering thread as stitching progresses.

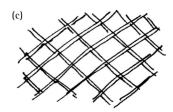
(c)

Ideas:

- Try gathering different types of fabric. Fine, transparent fabric will contract in size so would be suitable for small, delicate forms, whereas felt is heavy and bulky when gathered so that larger shapes would be more practical.
- Changing stitch direction will produce an uneven surface and help to create curves and make the gathered fabric distort. This could suggest the shape your form will eventually have.
- Stitch ribs or channels to the fabric first. Thread these with cord or fine wire to gather.
- Decorate the fabric first with hand or machine stitching before gathering.
- Combine a hard material with a soft one by making a rigid structure with wire or card and putting gathered fabric into the spaces.

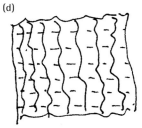
(d)

ABOVE: Gathers may be stitched in a variety of ways, such as: (a) spaced, (b) closed, (c) in two directions, (d) uneven length and placing of stitches.

LEFT: Dyed and printed, cotton fabric is gathered in circles to manipulate the surface.

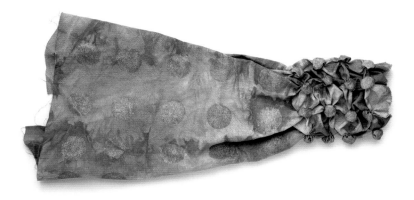

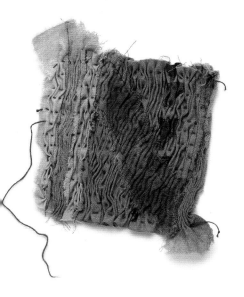

ABOVE: Fine fabrics are patched onto a fabric base and then gathered using a contrasting coloured thread.

RIGHT: A vessel, made from dyed and painted calico, has been gathered with stitches of uneven length. Small running stitches strengthen the top edge.

TUCKS AND PLEATS

The effects and usage of tucks and pleats are not dissimilar to gathers but are achieved differently and are fixed rather than flexible, unlike gathers that can be moved about. Small folds of fabric are stitched along their length, with tucks being very narrow and using very little fabric, while pleats are much wider and take up more fabric. They can be stitched randomly across the fabric, straight with the grain or on the cross, with even or uneven spacing, and they may vary in length. Stitching across the grain is interesting because the fabric begins to curl. This is a characteristic that can be harnessed to develop form. The fabric can be made to twist and turn, to roll and contort. There are many instances of this type of structure to be found in plants with a huge variety of stems, flowers, seedpods and leaves all having fibrous markings that could suggest tucks and pleats.

Ideas:

- Try making small pieces of tucked or pleated fabric and join them together by piecing and patching. The direction of the tucks can be varied depending on how the pieces are joined.
- Working with patches of various sizes enables the pieces to be further manipulated before joining.
- Try folding the pieces before joining, either along straight edges or corner to corner.

LEFT: Painted and dyed calico has been stitched into pleats and tucks and worked in several directions to give strength to the fabric. These help to support the shape of the vessel.

BELOW: An ear of sweetcorn, complete with its husk, has begun to dry out. The papery, protective covering with its lines of veining provides ideas for fine tucks in fabric. The texture of the inside and outside of the vessel can be contrasted by using the kernels as a lining and manipulated pin tucks for the outside surface. Quilting or beading would successfully evoke the rounded texture of the kernels.

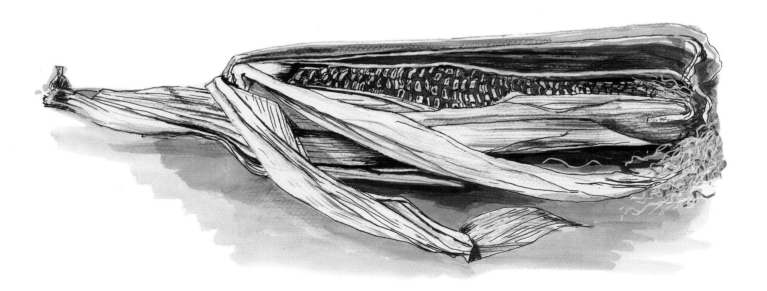

LEFT: Wrapping and gathering are combined in this soft, flexible vessel. Transparent fabrics were stitched to a felt base and then gathered in different directions to create a manipulated surface.

RIGHT: Stage felt is shaped with darts to form the basic shape of the bowl. Fine fabric is applied over the top and stitched. The outer surface is decorated with waste computer components.

BELOW: Darts can be made at the edge of fabric or placed more centrally. They may be straight or curved inwards or outwards. Each method produces a different effect and should be selected according to the shape of the piece.

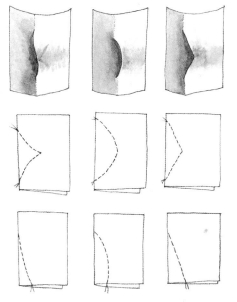

DARTS

Darts are usually employed in garment making to give the shaping that is required to fit a flat piece of fabric to a three-dimensional body. They can also be deployed when shaping fabric to create form and, in that context, are not unlike randomly placed tucks. When a rounded, stuffed shape is needed as a base for further embellishment, as in doll making, darts can be used for the necessary shaping.

Gussets also help to expand flat pieces of fabric. They may be straight in length or shaped with shallow curves or tapered at one or both ends.

RIGHT: Darts placed at either end of a piece of fabric result in a curve. Two or more of these shapes could be pieced together to create a rounded form as a basis for a vessel. The more darts included, the smoother the curve.

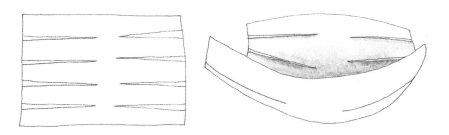

STUFFED SHAPES

Stylized birds and figures feature on embroideries worldwide and are often highly decorative with simple forms that are ideal for interpretation into stuffed sculptural shapes that can be richly embellished with stitching and beading. They could be developed into jewellery, with flatter shapes ideal for pendants and brooches.

- To create a three-dimensional bird goddess, several shapes will be necessary. Begin with a teardrop shape for the body, which will need a gusset to bulk it out. Fashion the gusset to taper to a point at both ends. Seam the two body shapes to the gusset and stuff with wadding. Add on another suitable shape for the head. A simple oblong of fabric is all that is needed. See the photograph opposite. Decorate with stitching and beading.

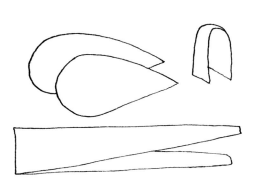 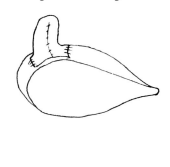

- The stylized peacock can be constructed from two semi-circles seamed to an oval gusset for the body. The head, neck and tail can be made by stuffing tubular ribbon of a suitable width. Surface details can be added once the shape is formed. Feet can be made from fine wires.

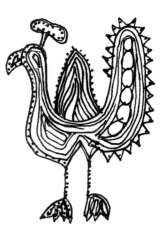

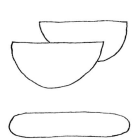 

- The bird could be made from two simple shapes seamed and stuffed as shown in the doll opposite. Set a wing shape into the seam. Once again, surface details can be added with stitch, fabric paint and beading.

TOP: An East Greek bird goddess perfume bottle, 640BC. Bird-like goddess figures are often found on Greek embroideries and some versions are linked to Russian pagan mythology.

MIDDLE: Northern Indian chain-stitch peacock made by the professional Mochi caste.

BOTTOM: Side view of a peacock from an Eastern Mediterranean Zoroastrian bridal shawl, 19th century.

ABOVE: Stuffed fabric shapes are a good starting point for further embellishment with stitching. More shapes and curves can be achieved by adding darts.

RIGHT: A Native American 'whimsy' from the Tuscarora reservation in New York State inspired this stuffed fabric doll. Two flat shapes were stitched together before stuffing, giving depth to the shape. Solid stitching decorates the surface.

HEATED FABRIC

Fabrics that can be heated for effect include Tyvek and acrylic felt.

Tyvek flowers

1 Make a base of copper wire. Cut lengths of about 20cm (8in) and twist together the first 8cm (3in). Open the rest out into a cup form.

2 Colour the Tyvek on both sides with ink, fabric paint or acrylic paint.

3 Stitch the Tyvek to the wire skeleton using a thread that will not burn, or you could use fine wire.

4 Using tweezers to hold the wired form, heat with a hot air tool until the material begins to melt and shrink on to the wire support. As the material shrinks away, holes will form and it will contort into itself.

Acrylic felt

1 Seam together machine-stitched fabric.

2 Melt with a heat tool to distort.

ABOVE A delicate seed head can be recreated with fine tucks on transparent fabric. Scaled-up fine wire – knitting with stitches dropped at intervals – can create the open, fragile wall of a vessel.

BELOW: Drawings of a datura flower look like rouched fabric or pleats. The curly tendril can be evoked with a wired edge. A fallen leaf, eaten away by insects, can be developed into a cutwork design.

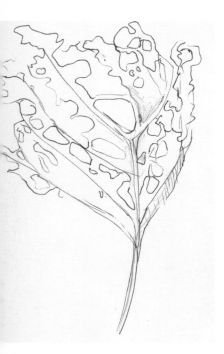

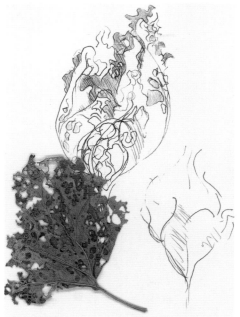

ABOVE: Fine-weight Tyvek fabric, painted on both sides, is stitched to a wire framework to make these small structures. They have been heated with a hot air tool for a few seconds until the fabric tightens around the frame and begins to melt and break into holes.

RIGHT: These small, shell-like structures have been made from wire spirals. Painted Tyvek fabric has been sewn on and heated, until the fabric becomes tight and breaks into holes.

ABOVE: Vessels knitted on four pins
using silk and paper string.
The shapes have been created by
adding on and casting off stitches.

KNITTING

Tubular knitting is ideal for creating a structure that can be embellished with stitching or beading. Thread or strips of fabric can be woven into the base shape or further shapes can be added on. A knitted fabric that you have made yourself is ideal for dipping in paper pulp as the open structure allows the fibres of the pulp to catch and adhere to it.

To make your knitted shape use four knitting needles or a circular one so that you end up with a tube as in making socks, so that you do not have a seam running through the shape. Stitches can be added or decreased as you wish in order to vary the width of the shape. Basic knitting is all you need but it would be possible to explore some of the many textured methods of knitting to enhance the surface.

Try knitting with fine wire for small, precious shapes. Wire can be rather stressful on the fingers so use the finest gauges, as they are easier to handle.

Ideas:
- Beads could be threaded on to the wire first before starting to knit.
- Combine thread with the wire and knit them together.
- Textured, bobbly yarns will add interest to the surface.
- Try knitting with paper string for a more robust form. Decrease or increase stitches as necessary for shaping.
- Stitch on to the knitted fabric after the shape has been made. Use buttonhole or chain stitch to add richness to the surface.
- Weave another thread through the knitting.

WEAVING

Weaving is a well-known basketry method of forming shape with numerous variations in technique and material. Wicker weaving, or stake and strand, involves a weft row passing over one warp or group of warps and under the next, over and under, over and under. The next row is reversed and the two rows repeated until an interlaced woven fabric is made.

Twinning is a weaving process using two or more flexible wefts simultaneously, that cross at intervals between the warps. Both the weaving and twinning methods are suitable areas for experimentation. In many parts of the world, temporary baskets are quickly made from local fibres. Simple and direct methods of construction are used, with beginnings and endings knotted together instead of being woven in and concealed. These ideas could be readily adapted to fabric with groups of ends being embellished with wrapping or stitching and beadwork.

Ideas:
- Work with narrow strips of torn fabric or wider ones that have been embellished with stitching first.
- Bands of wireform could be interlaced with another fabric.
- Try weaving machine cords and braids together.
- Combine silk paper with silk thread.
- Experiment with colour, using wefts of one colour, warps of another.
- Lash barbeque sticks or cocktail sticks together to make a free form. Tie or weave thread through and around the structure to

LEFT: This square box was inspired by the work of Ed Rossbach and Michael Brennand–Wood. A continous wrapped thread, used for a weft, and a rigid framework, used for the warp, are combined to form the sides of a cube. The MDF frame is drilled with small holes to allow the panels to be stitched to the structure.
(Nicola Oakley Watson)

RIGHT: A woven vessel constructed from strips of calico. The strips have been textured with tucks, couched string and cotton threads.

fill in some of the spaces. The whole piece can be dipped in paper pulp but if the shape is too big, the paper pulp can be poured over. It is best to stand it on a firm grid such as an oven shelf or something similar placed over a bowl or bucket, so that the surplus pulp can drain away and be saved for any future dippings.

Working with a former

Sometimes it is necessary to support the work while it is in progress. Flimsy or fragile materials will be much easier to work on if supported on a former. This is obviously only applicable when working by hand. If machine stitching is required, the work will need to be broken down into smaller units and combined after the machine stitching is complete.

In chapter 2 on page 32 you will find information about what can be used for a former.

PAPER

Paper can be used in pulp form to dip or pour over thread or fine fabric that has been wound on to or around a former. This could be a wire frame, a stone or a polystyrene shape, or any suitable found object. The thread could be any type but if it is matt and hairy, this characteristic enables the paper pulp to stick to it without flaking off when dry. The former should be wrapped in clingfilm first or coated in Vaseline to make removal possible. The resulting fabric is removed from the former when the pulp is dry, leaving a delicate shape that when joined with others may be built into a variety of larger forms. If the former is not flexible, for example, a stone, the pulped thread may have to be cut off and either stitched or glued together to repair the shape, if a whole shape is needed.

This method can be varied by using PVA glue or other fabric stiffeners instead of paper pulp to weld the fibres together.

Use silk, viscose or other fibres and lay over a former before stiffening them with cellulose solution or a specialist fabric stiffener. Cover the support with nylon fabric or thin plastic sheet to prevent the stiffening solution from adhering to it. Lay the fibres evenly over the former and cover with nylon net before applying the solution with a large brush. Leave it to dry. The fibres will harden and the plastic sheet and the net can be gently peeled away.

RIGHT: These vessels were formed by piecing together small pieces of machine embroidery worked on dissolvable fabric. These were placed over a mould shaped from oasis, a material commonly used for flower arranging. With some of the support material left behind, the fabric retained enough stiffness to support the shape. (Shireen Brickell)

BELOW: The shapes were tested with paper models before the vessel was built.

ABOVE: Calico, wrapped over a stone and stitched, is painted with fabric stiffener to harden it.

LEFT: This delicate, metalwork fairy was inspired by the colours and patterns of fish that inhabit coral reefs. The framework is constructed from machine-stitched wire, randomly wrapped with a finer decorative wire. She is dressed in sheer, iridescent fabrics and the bodice is embellished with metal thread. (Shirley Colbey)

Variations:

- Lay sheets of hand-made paper over wooden or other shapes and leave to dry where they will take on the shape of the former. They can then be cut and pieced to create larger shapes and can be embellished with stitching, beading or paint.
- Wet paper pulp can be moulded in the hand to create small shapes. Join these together in clusters by threading several together when the shapes are dry.
- Try joining small pieces of fibrous paper together to make a shape. Either overlap the edges of the pieces or make small seams by bringing the edges together and stitching firmly. The paper will need to be fairly flexible if traditional seams are employed. This method of building is easier to control if worked on a former but it is also possible to work without.

WIRE

In its many forms, wire is useful to give support to fabric.
In practice, I prefer to develop fabrics that will support themselves but many embroiderers are happy to incorporate wire into their work and there are times when other methods are not satisfactory.

Ideas:

- Wireform is a fine, woven material that can be manipulated into any shape. Try sandwiching it between layers of fabric and stitching by machine. Cut the resulting fabric into shape or scrunch it up into shape.
- Heating over a flame will improve the colour so that parts of the wireform can be left uncovered.
- Larger grades of wireform could be used as canvas and stitched using canvaswork stitches or other structured stitch techniques, such as blackwork or pattern darning, and then manipulated into shape.
- Lengths of wire can be threaded through channels stitched into fabric and then gathered to create fullness.
- Very fine jewellery wire can be couched on to the surface of fabric before being manipulated in other ways. It could be added at the same time as tucks are stitched.
- Fine wire can be covered in machine stitch and knitted to create shape or wrapped around a former.
- Scaling up, chicken wire can be bent and squeezed to create shape either freely or around a former. Spray paint it and add wrapping, beads or fragments of stitching or fabric.

Chapter 6
Beads

Beads are often seen only as an embellishment to surfaces, to add sparkle or a highlight, or in their own right as jewellery, but they can also be considered in the context of construction.

There are very many different methods of making beads, and this chapter shows some of them, both hard and soft, using various materials, but also gives some suggestions about ways of constructing with them, using individual beads as building blocks. The making of small beads is rather fiddly but many embroiderers like to make their own and enjoy the embellishing process using all those bits and pieces of stuff that they have within their collections of additions for embroidery.

BELOW: This combination of beads and other materials was discovered on a visit to the Pitt Rivers Museum in Oxford. The articles come from all over the world and show the diverse decorative skills used throughout history. Parts of shells have been threaded with fibres and brass teeth with strands of whale bone and large glass beads. A leopard's claw is mounted on a plaited cord. Leather and sticks, cowrie shells, wrapped grass, seeds, stones and feathers have all been crafted into beautiful objects for ceremonial, ritual and everyday use. This is a rich source of inspiration for making and using a wide variety of beads in contemporary items.

RIGHT: A framework of copper wire has been freely formed. Some spaces are filled with pieces of fine metal mesh, while others are filled with a combination of purchased beads and beads that have been wrapped with wire, all secured with fine wire.

As always, it is important to ensure that health and safety precautions are in place when using heat tools, fusing plastics and working with electrical equipment. Always follow the manufacturers' guidelines and instructions, and protect eyes with safety glasses when cutting wire. Secure wood to be cut by bracing with a clamp to a suitable worktop. Wear a dust mask when sanding wood or plastic and protect the work surface from heat and burning by using a soldering mat. I use an old kiln shelf to protect my tabletop as the ceramic material is designed to withstand considerable heat.

Requirements:
- Heat tool
- Soldering iron
- Mask
- Saw suitable for cutting wood
- Sandpaper
- Tweezers
- Scissors
- PVA glue
- Polyester stuffing/wadding
- Electric drill
- Jeweller's pliers
- Fine wires

The raw materials for making the beads may be fabrics, papers, wire, wood, clay or plastics, and threads for wrapping. Paint, thread for stitching, small seed beads and beading needles are needed for the embellishment.

Soft beads
STUFFED FABRIC TUBES

Fabric can be stitched into narrow tubes called *rouleaux*, which can be stuffed with wadding, cut and decorated to make beads. Any ribbon or braid that has a knitted tubular construction can be threaded with thick wool or have fine fabric pulled through it to pad it. Chopped up into small lengths with the ends sewn up, soft beads result, and these can then be decorated with stitch or small beads.

Method:
- Cut lengths of fine fabric, such as Habotai silk, into strips approximately 300mm (12in) long by 25mm (1in) wide. Fold the

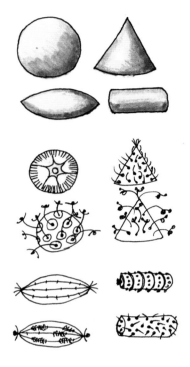

ABOVE: Basic shapes for beads embellished with thread, wire, tiny purchased beads and sequins.

ABOVE: A length of fabric is rolled up to make a bead. A long strip, even along its length, will give an oblong-shaped bead, while an elongated, triangular strip will result in a round shape, tapered at the ends.

strip in half lengthwise and machine down the long side about 3mm (⅛in) away from the edge. Make sure that you work a few stitches in reverse to fasten off your thread firmly.

- Turn the resulting tube inside out. This is not the easiest task to accomplish, but it can be done by first passing a strong thread through the tube with a bodkin and attaching it to the end of the tube.
- Roll the end of the tube back over a knitting needle. Help the fabric to turn by pulling the attached thread firmly and drawing the fabric over it. The turned tube can be stuffed with a small amount of polyester wadding or a thick thread passed through the channel using a bodkin. Cut the tube into short sections of about 50mm (2in) long. The ends can then be sewn up carefully, pushing the stuffing material into the cavity. This stuffed shape can then be further embellished with tiny seed beads or sequins to indent the surface.

Tubular ribbon can be treated in the same way by stuffing with thread or a narrow strip of fabric. Other small shapes, such as circles, ovals and cones, can be made and embellished with tiny beads or sequins.

BELOW: A collection of beads made using tiny, stuffed shapes and embellished with beads and sequins.

WRAPPED FABRIC

Small pieces of fabric can be made into free-formed beads by binding them into small bundles. This is an excellent way of using up all those fragments and tiny scraps of fabric from the ragbag that are too small to make anything else with. A range of fabric bits that are all slightly different in colour will look as if they are part of the same set when bound with coloured thread, which may be a blending colour or a contrast. Alternatively, scraps cut from the same piece of fabric, which could be one colour or patterned, may be wrapped with a variegated thread to give a mix of colour.

Method:

- Take a small bundle of fabric and lose the end of the wrapping thread in among it. Begin winding the thread around the fabric, manipulating the shape as you go. When you have enough thread wound around the fabric, thread up a needle so that you can fasten off.
- Pass the needle through the bead several times to secure.

BELOW: Fabric beads wrapped with calico and felt.

ABOVE: A stuffed shape, decorated with beads, forms the body of a spider. The legs are created by threading beads, made from embellished straws, onto pipe cleaners – wrapping the beads with a woolly thread gives a suitably hairy look to the spider's legs.

ROLLED FABRIC

Drinking straws, either the waxed paper type or plastic ones, can be used as a base for rolled fabric beads. If fabric is glued around them first, other decorative methods can be used to embellish them.

To make the beads, cut the straw into the required lengths; 30mm (1⅛in) is about the right size to begin with, giving about five or six pieces from each straw. You will be able to experiment with smaller or larger sizes when you have mastered the basic method. Prepare some fine cotton fabric the same width. Paste the fabric with PVA glue and lay the piece of cut straw on to it, matching the edges of fabric and straw. Roll up the straw with the pasted fabric to enclose. Roll the rest of the cut straws in the same way and leave to dry. These bead blanks can then be decorated. Try out any of the following methods.

Variations:
- Wrap with fine wires threaded with beads.
- Wrap with coloured thread, either randomly or evenly to produce a pattern of colour.
- Wrap with metallic thread and sequins.

- Paint with expandaprint or dimensional paint, heat to puff up.
- Gild with metallic foils.
- Wrap with shrink plastic.

Straw beads have a large hole running through them, making it possible to pass string or a thick thread such as leather thonging, wire or fine cane through them, to provide flexible, decorative lengths to build with.

Fabric can be also be rolled without having a length of straw through the middle. This is a better method if a smaller hole for threading is wanted. Thick fabric such as felt, Vilene or leather would be a suitable choice for chunky beads. Choose cotton or fine silk for fine beads.

Method:

1 Cut a length of fabric as wide as you wish your bead to be and about 200mm (8in) long. Wind the fabric around a thick darning needle or fine knitting needle and secure the end with a few small stitches if you want your bead to be shaped, in other words, fatter and rounded in the middle, cut your length of fabric in the shape of an elongated triangle. As you roll it up, it will increase in depth.

2 Fine, small beads can be made in the same way, but first add Bondaweb (fusible bonding medium) to the back of the fabric. It is then possible to roll up the fabric with the pressure of the iron. The Bondaweb secures the fabric. Make sure that you protect the iron and ironing surface with baking parchment.

Drinking straws can also be used for making beads without the fabric embellishment. Instead, dainty patterns can be imprinted on the surface of waxed paper straws using a soldering iron. You can burn tiny holes by resting the soldering iron lightly on the surface of the straw until it just pierces the paper. A light touch is needed, as it is all too easy to make holes that are too big. Organize the marks to make bands of pattern, combining dots and dashes in many different ways, taking care not to fragment the straw by making holes that are too big or too close together. The beads can be left white to show up the singed marks of the heat tool or could be painted with acrylics so that the marks show as surface texture. It is best to cut up the straw into bead lengths once the incising is complete. This will minimize the chance of burning the fingers.

Great care should be taken to keep fingers well away from the heated part of the iron and use tweezers to hold the straw. Work in a well-ventilated room and wear a mask to avoid breathing in smoke or fumes.

Compressed tissue balls can be treated in the same way, as can beads made from rolled paper. The tiny patterns and marks drawn from shells on page 13 would be an ideal source of inspiration for decorating them. The size of marks can be varied according to the pressure applied to the soldering iron. Paper beads can be quite dense if tightly rolled. I have had some success by holding the ends against a candle flame to singe them. Have a saucer of water beside you as you do this so that you can quickly extinguish any unwanted flame. I work directly in the sink so that there is no danger of anything catching fire. An over-sensitive smoke alarm will quickly detect too much enthusiasm so proceed with caution! You will need to dust off the ash that forms and you will find that the ends are slightly blackened. This will not matter because when the beads are painted the singed bits just merge in with the colour. They look very much like ceramic beads when complete.

BELOW: Paper balls and drinking straws, cut to the same length to make beads, have been decorated using a soldering iron to mark the surface.

Hard beads

Any material that can be shaped into small pieces and subsequently threaded can be utilized to make the hard type of bead.

CLAY

There are several types of clay on the market but the one that I favour is the air-dry type that dries hard and does not need baking in the oven. It is a good material to work with and unlike real clay does not give off any dust and does not dry the hands. It is very easy to mould and shape, and when dry can be drilled and sanded, painted and varnished.

Fimo clay is a type of thermoplastic resin. **Polyvinyl chloride**, a plastic polymer, is a heat-hardened resin and forms the basis of this type of modelling material. As there are some good books around that show how to use it, I will only mention it in passing here. As with air-dry clay, it has many good properties. The resin is already coloured, and can be easily modelled, with colours blended together for some striking effects. It can be cut and sanded when hardened and has a long shelf life. The difference is that it requires an oven for the hardening and curing process to be completed.

BELOW: A collection of beads made with air-dry clay. They are painted with acrylics and decorated using coloured gutta.

ABOVE: Shrink plastic beads that have been rolled and flattened.

PLASTICS

Any plastic that can be cut, melted and threaded is worth considering when making beads. Plastic packaging can often be recycled to form beads in the widest possible sense. Vacuum-packed products come encased in thick plastic that can be salvaged and utilized by cutting, piercing and melting. As with other materials in this category, safety issues are important, with the usual caution to be taken when heating or cutting.

Friendly plastic is meltable in hot water. Once softened, it can be moulded into shapes or stretched and rolled. It is possible to work with this material with a soldering iron too, spreading it on to fabric to make a raised surface, but this method can be rather heavy and ugly unless care is taken to blend it sensitively with fabric and stitching.

Shrink plastic reacts to heat. It can be coloured or marked with a wide range of pens, pencils and paints, and its main characteristic is that when heated it reduces to 45 per cent of its original size. It is wonderful for creating miniature patterns, drawn with a black or coloured fine liner pen or for reducing script to a tiny scale. Holes can be made for threading and joining, either before or after shrinking. It can be cut and rolled or made into any required shape.

Method:

1 Prepare the plastic by colouring the rough side with inks or coloured pencils. If neither side is rough you will need to sand the surface with a fine grade of sand paper to give a key for your colour. However, you could draw with a permanent spirit-based pen that is designed to work on acetates and then there is no need to roughen the surface.

2 Cut the plastic into pieces or shapes and make holes for joining by
using a hole punch or passing a large darning needle through.
Remember that the plastic will shrink by almost half so make the
holes large enough to take account of this and the shapes not so
small that you are unable to work with them.

3 The plastic can be put into an electric oven heated to 175°C
(350°F/ gas mark 3). If your oven is a fan-assisted type, you should
switch off this facility as your plastic will fly around the oven and
may get deposited on parts of the oven surface where it is
impossible to remove. Place the plastic on a baking tray lined with
tin foil. It will take only a few minutes before the plastic begins
to curl and twist. Leave it until it begins to uncurl and flatten.
When flat, take out of the oven using an oven glove, place on to a
firm surface and immediately place under a piece of wood or a
tablemat to press flat for a few moments. This prevents the plastic
having a slight kink or curve to the surface. It will cool very
rapidly so it is essential to work very fast. You need to prepare
your working space in advance and have everything you need to
hand. If the plastic cools before it is quite flat, heat it up again to
make it pliable. Alternatively, if you want to roll the plastic, do it
while it is still pliable.

I prefer to work with a heat tool, as I am not keen on using my
domestic oven for anything other than cooking food. I also feel
much more in control of the material as I can work with one piece
at a time. I work on an ironing board, protecting the surface with
baking parchment. To shrink the plastic with a heat tool, use
tweezers to hold the plastic and prevent your fingers being too near
the heat source. Direct the heat tool at the plastic until it begins to
melt. Don't panic when you see the plastic curling up. Just keep
moving the heat about and very soon the plastic will begin to
uncurl. Once again, wait until it is flat, turn off the heat and press
down with a block of wood to completely flatten the plastic, which
will now be very small.

Ideas:
• Thread strips of colour through another piece of plastic.
• Weld previously shrunken shapes on to plastic.
• Join shapes together with fine wire before melting.

TYVEK
Tyvek is made from very fine, high-density polyethylene fibres. It has
the characteristics of paper, film and fabric all rolled into one
material. There are two types, one that is more like stiff paper and is

ABOVE: Ideas for beads drawn from Ernst Heackel's book *Art Forms in Nature*.

commonly used for envelopes, and a soft type that is more like fabric. This type can be effectively used to make rolled beads. The uses of this material are covered very thoroughly in other publications, so suffice it to say here that it can be painted, rolled and then distorted with a heat tool to melt through the layers.

WOOD

Lengths of dowel and square mouldings of various dimensions can be bought in your local DIY store. When sawn into pieces and small holes drilled through the middle for threading, these wooden beads can be painted with acrylic paints or dyed with fibre-reactive (procian) dyes. Add further decoration using a permanent pen or dimensional paint before polishing. Small pieces of coloured fabric could be glued on to the surface.

Balsa wood is very easy to work with. Hobby shops stock a wide variety of shapes and sizes of balsa that can be easily cut, shaped and drilled. It is quite soft so it is possible to incise patterns with a soldering iron and the surface will take any type of paint, ink or polish.

ABOVE: A collection of beads made with a wire-coiling gizmo.

LEFT: Asian bridal jewellery provides the inspiration for this machine-stitched vessel. Stitched wireform panels are decorated with layers of Lasertran, areas of knotted gimp and beading. The panels are held in place with machined wire and wrapped metal foil beads. The base was made and attached separately, with rolled metal beads forming the feet. (Amarjeet Nandrha)

WIRE

Wire is a versatile medium for beads as it offers so much variety. The thickness or gauge of wire determines how easily it can be manipulated. The thicker the wire and the larger the gauge number, the more difficult it is to work. It is useful to understand how wire is measured so that when ordering wires from a catalogue you know what you are buying. Actual measurement in thousandths of an inch or in millimetres is the standard method, with the gauge number increasing as the wire gets thicker. For embroidery purposes, wires at the fine end of the range are most useful. Fine, coloured wires can be rolled and twisted or made into specific shapes by wrapping around a jig. This can be simply made by knocking short pieces of fine dowel into drilled holes in a piece of soft wood to make a pattern of pegs. Fine wire can be wound around the pegs to make wire shape. The benefit of using a jig is that you can make exact repeats of a shape.

Rolled wire beads can be made by winding fine wire around a knitting needle. However, if you are going to make a quantity of them, which is likely to be the case if you are constructing with them, it is much easier on the fingers if you make them on a coiling gizmo. This is done by feeding wire on to the winding gizmo to give a length of uniformly sized rolled wire that looks like a spring. This can be cut into lengths for threading. Variations can be created by threading a thicker wire through the fine rolled wire and then rewinding. The fine wire is wrapped around the thicker one. Great variety can be had by combining two or more colours of fine wire and winding them together. Try these combinations.

Variations:
- Two fine coloured wires wrapped around a thicker wire of a different colour.
- Machine stitch over the wire before winding.
- Thread small beads on to the wire before winding. These may be evenly distributed along the length of the winding or may be separated at intervals by a straight length of wound wire.
- Thread bugle beads on to the wire before winding. This creates a square pattern to the wound wire.
- Stretch out a length of rolled wire before threading on to a thick wire and winding.
- Wind a machine cord or thick thread with a fine wire.
- Pass a wire through a length of tubular cord before winding.

THREADED COMMERCIAL BEADS
This category is well served with a great variety of books on the subject, covering the many techniques associated with beading that I do not intend to repeat here. I have included useful titles in the Further reading section, as some methods, such as peyote stitch, square stitch or netting techniques, are worth combining with collections of individually made beads as I have described – rolled or wrapped, hard or soft.

Building with beads

Once you have made a collection of beads, it is possible to use them to make three-dimensional forms. Bowls, vessels and boxes of various kinds can be made. Sculptural forms or decorative embellishments can be made for bags, hats or jewellery. Creating in response to a design theme can lead to unusual and unexpected results. Artefacts from around the world can be seen in museums or on your travels, and may inspire all kinds of creations. Try some of these methods of building with beads.

ABOVE: Inspired by a Moroccan saddle blanket, this richly decorated box is constructed from a simple wooden frame covered with scrim. The beads, made from Tyvek, wood and metal and combined with purchased bells, are threaded across the frame. (Karen Staples)

ON A FORMER

All the shapes listed below can give support to beads during construction, whether they are being threaded or linked together in other ways. It will, of course, be necessary to consider how the former is to be removed when its job is done.

Ideas:

- Polystyrene balls, either round or oval shaped for bowls and basket shapes. Polystyrene is easy to pin into for support.
- Crumpled newspaper or card tubes salvaged from paper towels.
- Wooden forms, such as logs or branches.
- Clay shapes.
- Stones.
- Bowls or baskets.
- Stuffed fabric shapes, such as an ironing board sleeve or a shape specially made.

THREAD WITH WIRE

Beads threaded on to wire can be made into shapes that are joined together in various ways, including tied, wired or wrapped.

The vessel shown was constructed by freely wrapping copper wire round and round, criss-crossing it over and over until a simple form was made. (See chapter 4, Free-form building.) Junctions of wires were bound with fine wire to support the shape. The spaces in between were then filled with rolled wire beads combined with a selection of commercially made beads and threaded on to fine wire. Some spaces were filled in with metal mesh and others were filled

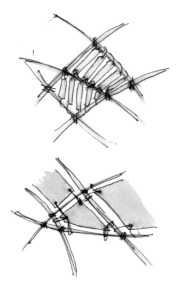

ABOVE: The space that is left between wires that have been wrapped around a former could be filled with rolled beads or shrink-plastic shapes.

LEFT: A sample showing how small commercial beads can be threaded together and supported – in this case, by a smooth, rounded stone. When the beading is complete enough to support itself, the form can be removed and further embellishment worked onto the surface or on the edge.

RIGHT: A wire armature provides support for a doll, with wrapped beads forming the skirt. A wire tiara tops the turban.

using a fine metallic thread and a needlelace stitch. Care was taken to ensure that the form was stable and balanced. The base section was constructed from thick copper wire wound around a card tube to form the shape. Fine wires and threaded beads were worked into the spaces in the same way as for the upper shape. This shape was then securely bound to the upper section of the vessel with fine wire.

This method of wrapping a length of wire round and round until a shape is formed can be adapted by using thick cord or torn fabric, but a former will be needed when a soft material is used to support the shape while work is in progress. Try threading beads you have made on to the cord or torn strips of fabric.

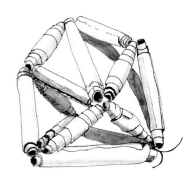

ABOVE: Rolled beads can be scaled up and threaded with strong, waxed thread or wire to create open structures.

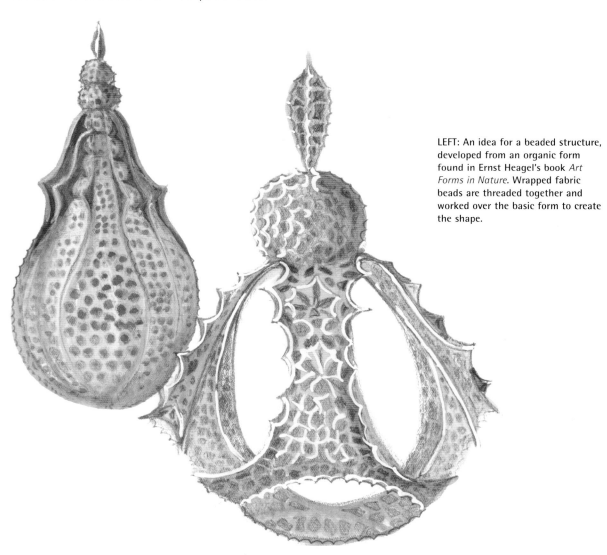

LEFT: An idea for a beaded structure, developed from an organic form found in Ernst Heagel's book *Art Forms in Nature*. Wrapped fabric beads are threaded together and worked over the basic form to create the shape.

ABOVE: Coloured fabric is wrapped to
form beads, which are then threaded
with wire. The accompanying
drawing (see left) shows the plan for
the arrangement of the beads.

SEW TOGETHER

Sew rolled or wrapped fabric beads together to make a larger
'fabric'. Placed over a former to support, a vessel or bowl shape can
be made.

THREAD ON TO WOODEN RODS

Beads that have a large hole can be threaded on to a length of
narrow dowel or barbeque sticks. These could be joined together by
wiring, gluing or binding with thread.

AN ARMATURE

A simple armature can be constructed by drilling a small hole into a
suitable block of wood. Push a length of thick wire into the hole
making sure that it goes into the wood for at least 2.5cm (1in).
If you squeeze some glue into the hole first it will give the wire a
firmer bond. Further wires can be attached to the first as necessary,
depending on what the final form is to be.

ABOVE: Rolled beads can be combined with beads that have been wound with wire and threaded to make a vessel.

LEFT: A vessel formed from wrapped fabric and straw beads threaded onto wires. These are inserted into a block of wood to give a stable support to the shape.

Vessel using soft beads

Requirements:
- A block of wood for the base
- Strong glue
- Drill
- Stiff coloured wire
- A collection of beads
- Purchased beads
- Fine wire covered with machine stitch
- Needle and strong thread

1 Prepare a wooden base by painting or waxing, and then drill small holes around the top edge.

2 Cut lengths of thick wire and place them into the holes that have had strong contact glue squirted into them. Leave to harden.

3 Make a collection of beads using covered, wrapped straws and wrapped fabric bundles.

4 Thread the wrapped straws on to the wire uprights and link these with wrapped fabric bundles horizontally, adding purchased beads for extra embellishment as you go.

5 Decorate the top edge with thick wire twisted with a machined fine wire that has small beads attached.

Chapter 7
Finishing techniques

Finishing techniques need to be carefully considered and should be in keeping with the essence of a piece. Whether to choose a decorative method or something simple but effective will depend on the type of work and what inspired it. Function may rule out embellishment and demand practicality. Simple bindings that do the job but do not draw attention to themselves may be the answer or perhaps a stitched edge that brings the piece to a satisfactory full stop is required. On the other hand, if the piece of work is purely decorative, then it is possible to develop an edge that takes the ornament still further and a vigorous, flamboyant approach may be what is needed.

When considering vessels or boxes it is the tops and bottoms that demand attention. The meeting of the vertical plane with the horizontal makes an important statement and mounting your vessel on to a plinth or on feet that raise it off the horizontal surface by just a small amount can make quite a difference to the elegance of the piece. From a practical point of view, it is also a method of dealing with any irregularity to the base of a piece that is uneven or has a wobble.

Edges and rims

Edges and rims need to reflect the theme and essence of a piece. The subject matter selected as inspiration may suggest a suitable finish and research may be needed to find something that is appropriate. If the work is organic in style, the chosen finish may be ragged or hairy, softly frayed or fringed. But if geometry is the nature of the piece, then a neat, crisp, calculated, clean-cut edge may be more appropriate.

SOFT EDGES
Choose layering, fringing, stitching, ruffles, soft bindings, machine-made lacy effects, disintegrated by heat treatments.

RIGHT: Having looked at the engineering of bridges, railways and spiral staircases and the effects that weathering has on metal, this *papier-mâché* bowl was inspired by a rusty rivet. The shape was developed using *papier-mâché* and a beach ball, and a pieced, fabric rim is enhanced with machine vermicelli stitch and sorbello. (Alisa West)

HARD EDGES

Choose crisply cut, turned edges, machined rows of stitching, bonding or beading.

Bases, supports and feet

It is essential for vessels or free-formed pieces to stand firmly and not to be wobbly and topple over. Forms that taper sharply to the base may need to rest on or in a support, or the base may need to be weighted in order to give the required stability. Sometimes the look of the finished item can be enhanced by raising it up off the horizontal surface with added feet.

Incorporating a hard material, wood being the obvious choice, it is possible to achieve a more acute angle to the way that a vessel stands. The base could be built up at one side to project the piece forward and, if weighted with a piece of metal, or sand if it is hollow, it would be stable.

WIRE ARMATURE

A wire armature can be simply made by drilling a suitably sized hole into a block of wood and pushing a thick wire into the hole. Make sure that it penetrates the wood by a sufficient amount so that it doesn't fall out. How much depends on the size of the piece, but a

ABOVE LEFT: The edge of the bowl is made from a wide, metal, tubular braid. This is stuffed with metallic fabric and wrapped with beaded wire.

ABOVE RIGHT: The edge of this Tyvek structure is decorated with fine wires and tiny beads, and is evocative of the stamen found at the centre of a flower.

RIGHT: This item, entitled 'The Dragon's Lexicon', was constructed from garden wire, covered with dyed fabrics, and wrapped with fine wire and metallic threads. Further decoration, in the form of letters and other symbols made from wrapped wire, were worked into the mesh. Wrapped pipe cleaners form the feet and the dragon's head is made from air-dry clay, painted with metallic paints and mounted onto wrapped garden wire.
(Carolyn Holding)

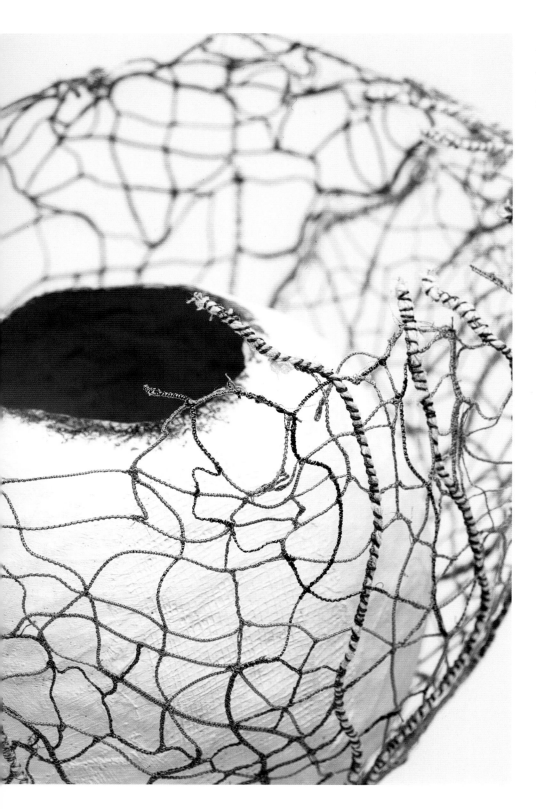

LEFT: A dried flower head inspired this bowl shape, made from paper and scrim set into a wire cage. The inside of the bowl was shaped around a mould, then painted and sanded smooth. Fine wire was machine stitched into an open, lacy mesh and used to surround the inner sphere.

depth of at least 30mm (1⅛in) should be a guide. Large pieces would need more. Some strong glue may be squeezed into the hole first before pushing the wire into it.

WOOD BASE

Wood can be cut to any size and shape, and can provide weight and height to a finished piece. A textile can be sewn to the wood if necessary. Drill small holes into the wood so that it is possible to pass a needle and thread through and firmly stitch the textile in place using a strong waxed thread. Alternatively, the textile base could be stuck to a wooden base using strong PVA glue. However, I would only recommend this method if stitching is not an option.

CARD BASE

A base can be constructed from thick card such as grey board. Cut out the top, bottom and sides, and glue together using tissue paper to strengthen joints. Any irregularities in cutting or measuring can be filled with the tissue and a very strong finish can be achieved. The resulting base can be sanded down ready for painting or covered with fabric. The textile can be attached to the base by gluing or stitching.

WIRE SUPPORT

Thick wire can be used to create a cradle or stand for a textile that may be either shaped to a point or have too small a base for it to be able to stand on its own. This idea could be developed with fabric and stitch too, so that the piece and its support are interdependent.

FEET

Making feet can be a good way of stabilizing a piece of work that is a bit wobbly. If it is supported on three small feet this is often enough to even out small discrepancies in what should be a flat plane. There are a number of methods that could be chosen and the nature of the piece of work will dictate the choice.

- Wooden cupboard knobs are useful. Small ones could be glued, providing the surface of the textile is smooth. Larger ones will need to be screwed in place using brass screws and putting a false base inside the vessel. This may be thin ply, MDF or thick card. Reinforce the inside of the textile base with a small piece of kid or leather to prevent wear and slippage.

ABOVE: The square box stands on a raised plinth. A cardboard base is covered with fabric and decorated with fabric paint and a machine-stitched braid.

- Suitable beads or buttons can be purchased or made.
- Padded button shapes or stuffed shapes made from Vilene or calico could be stitched to the base.
- Air-dry clay could be used to form feet. Remember to add small holes so that it is possible to sew them on. They can be painted to fit in with the colour and decoration of the piece.

Lids

Vessels or boxes that you make may need a lid to complete the design. Consideration should be given as to how the lid of the box might be prevented from sinking into the opening and how it is to be opened. Knobs and loops or tabs may make it easier to open and close the box, and prevent wear to the surface. The lid may be detached from the body of the box or perhaps it could be hinged. Try the following methods.

- A strip of fabric can be added around three sides of the lid, increasing the size so that it overlaps the top edge.
- Stitch a thick cord to the top of the three inside edges of the opening. This will give a narrow ledge for the lid to rest on and

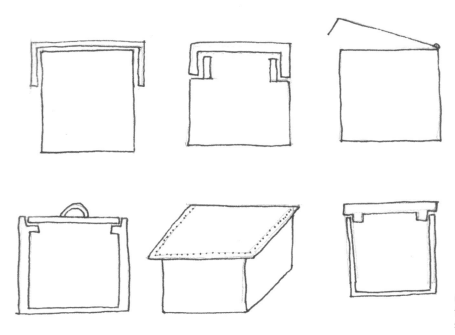

LEFT: Lids for boxes or vessels can take many forms. The diagram shows some variations.

RIGHT: A detail showing the lid of a casket box. Shapes placed at the corners fit over the body of the box and into the space between the circles on the sides. Inside, a raised lining drops into the opening space to give a snug fit.

ABOVE: A hinge is made from two pieces of fabric by folding back the opposing edges to form a channel. Stitch the channel securely, then cut out and remove alternate segments so that the two edges interlink. Pass a barbeque stick through the channels to enable the hinge to open and close. The channel should fit tightly around the stick otherwise the fabric will move so much that the hinge won't work properly.

the outside edges of lid and box meet without overhang. This could be a drop-in lid if the support was around all four sides of the box or could remain attached to the box on one edge.

- Increase the size of the lid so that it extends beyond the top of the box and rests on the top edge.
- Fit a cord to the underside of the lid. This can give a snug fit that will hold the box shut. The outside edge of the lid should sit on the top edge of the box flush with the side wall.
- Create a hinge from kid or Vilene, making sure that where it overlaps the surface of the vessel or box it fits with the design and is not just placed without regard to its surroundings.

Conclusion
A personal perspective

Working in three dimensions has great potential but needs much careful consideration. As a former potter making three-dimensional forms spontaneously on the potter's wheel, working with fabric and thread has presented rather different problems in terms of the treatments of material, although the design considerations remain largely the same. I have found the experience of working in clay for many years has enriched my practice with fabric and thread. Techniques of forming overlap between the two disciplines, so I have continued to use the same methods. Slab building in clay translates very well into working with flat pieces of textile, while coiling methods in both clay and fabric are not too dissimilar. Free-form work is comparable, too, as it is possible to add and take away material whether it is clay or fabric. When it comes to decoration, the effect of surface is much the same, accepting that one will be hard and the other relatively soft. It is only the methods of achieving the surface that are obviously significantly different and the problems of firing and mixing glazes are welcome in their

BELOW: Wrapping techniques are used to create deep pockets. Fine, machine-stitched cords are coiled to form tiny vessels, and make great ideas for storage. Cotton fabrics, often recycled, are used throughout.

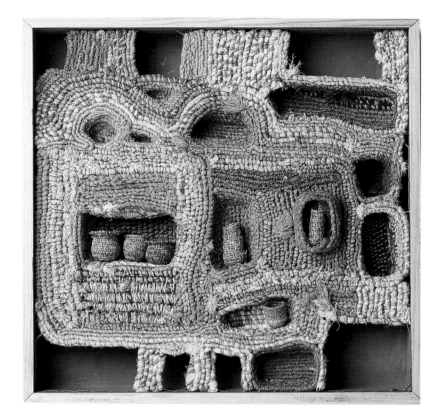

RIGHT: Wrapping, binding and coiling are used to create more pockets and pots. Recycling old fabrics brings new life to waste materials. The techniques used add strength to worn out fabric.

absence. In addition, the colour you see is the colour you get when working with fabric and thread, and the excitement when opening the kiln to see what has happened is replaced with the anticipation of seeing what colour your fabric is when it emerges from the dye bath. At least, that is the way it is when I have a dyeing session.

Personal design themes remain constant over time. Organic subjects usually take precedence, with landscape and natural forms continuing to inspire me. A busy teaching programme demands that techniques cover all areas across the range of hand and machine stitching, but a special interest in three-dimensional and sculptural embroidery has always been dominant. My work explores ideas based on the structures and rhythms of the natural world. Recent work explores form in a more personal way, with these ideas providing inspiration for the interpretation of the mind's storage system. So much of daily life revolves around layers of activity, separate packages of stuff that is divided into compartments. Things to remember, for another time, or things to do when conditions are right, get filed away in the far recesses of the mind, layer on layer. Fragments of information are stacked up and stored for future reference and action. These pockets of information are the focus for visual imagery that expresses the labyrinth of mental storage systems.

I hope that readers will be inspired to explore their own personal themes in three dimensions using some of the methods described in this book. There is much scope for experimentation and the ideas given here are offered merely as an introduction.

Resources

Suppliers

UNITED KINGDOM

Art Van Go
The Studios
1 Stevenage Road
Knebworth SG3 6AN
01438 814946
www.artvango.co.uk

Creative Beadcraft (Elles & Farrier)
Unit 2
Asheridge Business Centre
Asheridge Road
Chesham
Buckinghamshire HP5 2PT
01494 778818
www.creativebeadcraft.co.uk

Fibrecrafts
Old Portsmouth Road
Peasmarsh
Guildford
Surrey GU3 1LZ
01483 565800
www.fibrecrafts.com

The Scientific Wire Company
18 Raven Road
London E18 1HW
020 8505 0002
www.scientificwire.com

The Smithfield Gallery
Unit 9
Lake Enterprise Park
Caton Road
Lancaster LA1 3NX
01524 762883
www.smithfieldgallery.co.uk

Stitch'n'Craft
Swans Yard Craft Centre
High Street
Shaftesbury
Dorset SP7 8JQ
01747 852500
www.stitchncraft.co.uk

Alec Tiranti Ltd
High Street
Theale
Reading
Berkshire RG7 5AR
0118 930 2775
www.tiranti.co.uk

Whaleys (Bradford) Ltd
Harris Court
Great Horton
Bradford
West Yorkshire BD7 4EQ
01274 576718
www.whaleys-bradford.ltd.uk

AUSTRALIA AND NEW ZEALAND

The Thread Studio
6 Smith Street
Perth
WA 6000
Australia
+61 (0)9 227 1561
www.thethreadstudio.com

Anne's Glory Box
60–62 Beaumont Street
Hamilton
NSW 2303
Australia
+61 2 4961 6016
www.annesglorybox.com.au

Craft Supplies
31 Gurney Road
Belmont
Lower Hutt
New Zealand
www.dianaparkes.co.nz

Further reading

The Art of Manipulating Fabric, Colette Wolff, Krause Publications, 1996

Sources of Inspiration, Carolyn Genders, A & C Black, 2002

Textile Perspectives in Mixed-media Sculpture, Jac Scott, The Crowood Press, 2003

Principals of Form and Design, Wucius Wong, John Wiley & Sons Inc, 1993

Design Synectics: Stimulating Creativity in Design, Nicholas Roukes, Davies Publications Inc, 1988

Basic Design: Dynamics of Visual Form, Maurice De Sausmarez, Herbert Press, 2002

Experimental Embroidery, Edith John, BT Batsford, 1976

Textile Techniques in Metal: For Jewellers, Textile Artists and Sculptors, Arline Fisch, Lark Books, 2002

Embroidered Textiles: Traditional Patterns from Five Continents, Sheila Paine, Thames and Hudson Ltd, 1995

Nature as Designer, Bertel Bager, Frederick Warne & Co, 1971

Surfaces for Stitch, Gwen Hedley, BT Batsford, 2004

Creative Bead Weaving: A Contemporary Guide to Classic, Off-loom Stitches, Carol Wilcox Wells, Lark Books, 2000

Polymer Clay Basics: Techniques, Tools and Projects, Monica Reston, Sterling Publishing Co., 2001

Papermaking for Basketry and other Crafts, Lynn Stearns (Editor), Lark Books, 1992

Felt Without Seams: Making Hollow Forms, Sheila Smith, Felt by Design, 2002

The Handmade Paper Book, Angela Ramsey, Storey Books, 1999

Art Forms in Nature, Ernst Haeckel, Dover Publications, 1974

Index

Aboriginal *Pukumani* 44, 45
Air-dry clay 102,120
Armature 110, 113, 118
Aztec 45
Baking parchment 30, 100
Badger, Bertel 12
Balsa wood 27, 105
Beads 40, 56, 69, 76, 82, 87, 88, 93, 94, 98, 99, 115
Binding 56, 65, 72, 113, 116
Bondaweb 30, 46, 100
Calico 48, 72
Cane 32
Card 31,32, 39, 45, 60, 76, 110
Cellulose solution 90
Clay 28, 102, 110, 120, 122
Coiling 54, 58, 60, 122
Coiling gizmo 30, 107, 108
Construction 60, 110, 112
Cord winder 30
Cutting equipment 29
Cutwork 50
Cylinder 45, 46, 47, 48, 74
Darts 53, 70, 81
Decoration 31, 54, 69, 73
Design brief 12
Dimensional paint 100
Dowel 107, 113
Drafting materials 31
Felt 23, 26, 30, 48, 53, 70, 73, 84
Fibre-reactive (procian) dyes 105
Fimo 28, 102
Finishings 62, 116
Former 32, 46, 60, 90, 93, 110, 112
Foundation 54, 58, 62
Free form 50, 65, 122

Function 23, 69, 116
Gathering, gathers 70, 74, 75, 76, 79
Geometric 14, 34, 35
Goethe 23
Gusset 81, 82
Hand stitch 40, 62, 69, 76, 82, 87, 88, 93, 122
Heackel, Ernst 105, 112
Hessian 26, 73
Hot-air tool 30, 84, 85, 96, 104
Jig 107
Knitting 70, 84, 86, 93
Leather 26, 100, 120
Machine stitch 32, 40, 48, 49, 53, 62, 65, 90, 93, 108, 118, 123
Manipulative techniques 23, 53, 70, 74
Millinery wire 28
Mind map 15, 16
Model/mockup 18, 23
Native American 'whimsy' 83
Networks 35, 42
Nymo 26
Organdie 73
Organza 73
Paper 70, 87, 96
Paper pulp 66, 69, 87, 90, 93
Piecing/patching 70, 79
Pitt Rivers Museum 94
Plant material 20, 21, 65
Plastics 24, 28, 53, 96, 103
Plinth 116
Polystyrene 32, 110
PVA glue 28, 46, 73, 90, 120
Repetition 34, 4, 53
Rouleaux 96

Scrap store 24
Scrim 72
Shape 42, 45, 46, 50, 60, 62, 65, 66, 76, 81, 82, 87, 97
Shells 16, 17, 101
Sinemay 73
Sketchbook 12, 18, 30
Slices 34, 47
Soldering iron 30, 96, 100, 101
Space 14, 34, 42, 49, 66, 110
Spiral 13, 16, 17, 85
Stage felt 24
Stiffening solutions 28, 29
Straws 99, 100, 101, 115
Stevens, Peter 18
Structure 10, 14,18, 23, 32, 43, 47, 50, 53, 69, 79, 85, 87
Styrofoam 32
Tissue paper 73, 120
Transparent fabric 23
Tubular ribbon 27, 82, 96, 97, 108
Tucks 70, 79, 81, 93
Tyvek 84, 85, 104
Unit shape 34, 35, 36, 40, 53
Vilene 2, 39, 48, 49, 50, 53, 100, 120, 121
Weaving 66, 70, 87
Wrapping 54, 56, 57, 60, 62, 88, 93, 98, 99, 110, 115
Wire 24, 27, 28, 29, 53, 56, 65, 69, 76, 82, 84, 85, 87, 107, 11, 115, 118
Wireform 28, 88, 93
Wood 2, 93, 96, 105, 113, 115, 118, 120